Coining for Capital

Coining for Capital

Movies, Marketing, and the Transformation of Childhood

JYOTSNA KAPUR

RUTGERS UNIVERSITY PRESS
New Brunswick, New Jersey, and London

Library of Congress Cataloging-in-Publication Data

Kapur, Jyotsna.
  Coining for capital : movies, marketing, and the transformation of
childhood / Jyotsna Kapur.
      p. cm.
  Includes bibliographical references and index.
  ISBN 0-8135-3592-1 (alk. paper) — ISBN 0-8135-3593-X (pbk. : alk.
paper)
      1. Children—United States—social conditions—20th century. 2. Child
consumers—United States. 3. Advertising and children—United States.
4. Children in motion pictures. I. Title.

  HQ792.U5K36 2005
  305.23'09'04—dc22

                                                        2004023481

A British Cataloging-in-Publication record for this book is available from
the British Library

Manufactured in the United States of America

*For Suhaila, Nilim, and their grandparents,
Narinder and Satinder*

Contents

Acknowledgments

This book owes its existence to my two children, Suhaila and Nilim, who have shared with me endless hours of watching children's films and television, reading "Made in" labels in stores, and, most of all, helped bring home in a visceral sense the vulnerability of all children. In the first few quiet moments that follow their falling asleep, I, like other parents, have felt that poignant sense of gratitude from knowing that our children are secure, for we all know that we can never take for granted the security we provide our children. How can we, when we know that there is no safety net for children if the adults who by mere accident of birth are responsible for them become incapable of taking care of them? When we know that an abandoned child has little value on the streets of our world, while the young lives in our homes are infinitely invaluable? It is to that agonizingly tender awareness—one that I share with my own parents, other parents, and all adults who have loved a child—that I dedicate this book.

Writing *Coining for Capital* has not been easy, because the pessimism I feel about the future hangs in a fine balance with the optimism that is necessary to and also a gift from loving children. Here I was helped enormously by my dissertation committee, Professors Chuck Kleinhans, Manjunath Pendakur, and Tom Gunning, who were unwavering in pointing out the contradictions in both my analysis and what I analyzed. All three will find their insights, knowledge, and experiences cooked together in these pages. It is to them that I owe the mix of critical theory, political economy, and the connections between cinema, modernity, and consumer culture that has informed my understanding of children's consumer culture. Chuck's sharp humor and distrust of all sorts of "authorities," backed by an unwavering commitment to theory that would transform the structural exploitation of class, gender, race, and sexuality, was an anchor among the changing fads of postmodern, poststructuralist thinking. He has lived the longest with this work, helping articulate answers when even the questions were only half-formed. I was to turn to Manju Pendakur for lessons in political economy and the systemic nature of capitalist expansion. Luckily for me, Manju is now at Southern Illinois University, where I teach, and I need walk just a few yards to ask questions, not just about the political economy of the media industry but about life itself as it is these days. I will always be grateful to Tom for insisting that I need "to go back and look at texts" rather than read them solely to prove a theory. That lesson, along with Tom's work in early cinema and consumer culture, has served me well.

The seeds of this work, the Marxist-feminist theory that forms its core, go back to my days at Delhi University in the 1980s and my teachers there, particularly Randhir Singh, Sumit Sarkar, and Tanika Sarkar. The conviction that in imagining an alternative world we should put children first was made palpably clear for me by Barry John, a children's drama teacher with whom I worked in Delhi.

Of the people who have spoken with me and helped clarify my thinking, I would like to thank Amy Beer, Judy Hoffman, Julia Lesage-Hyun suk Seo, Jeffrey Skoller, and Usha Zaccharias, who remained only an email or phone call away. At Southern Illinois University, I would like to thank my students, who will recognize in the following pages our class discussions, which helped me to better articulate the ideas expressed here. I would especially like to thank Shannon Petrello for the cover image, Hwa-young Youn for research assistance, and Sudesh Balan for collecting the film frames. My colleagues Lilly Boruszkowski, Mike Covell and Jan Roddy mentored me in teaching and in combining the obligations of academic work with one's own writing. Both sent my way news clippings and other bits of information that would help this project along. Best of all, they were also there to play and celebrate, and not always for a reason. Thanks are also due to Kevin Koron for all his help with the technical details of this work, to the Department of Cinema and Photography and the College of Mass Media and Media Arts for course releases, and for the encouragement and inspiration I received from Manjunath Pendakur, our college dean. Thanks are also due to Leslie Mitchner, my editor at Rutgers University Press, for believing in this project, to Nicole Manganaro who saw it through production, and to Bobbe Needham, whose close reading made this text immeasurably better to read.

As always, there is a net of friends and comrades with whom the boundaries between work and home collapse, in whose absence it would be difficult to get through life, let alone write a book. Here are people who have helped with child care, shared stories and jokes, helped find work, listened to my troubles, gone on protest marches, and shared moments that are too numerous to recount. To Ronald Loeffler, who unconditionally opened his home and life to me and stuck by the ups and downs of mine, I will always be grateful. Roja Pendakur's thoughtful consideration and concern helped nurture both my body and mind. The Southern Illinois Peace Coalition, particularly the friends I made there, Georgeann Harzog, Celeste Williams, and Heather Howley, helped sustain a sense of optimism in our ability to act collectively against injustice. Mike Covell, who can farm in the morning, teach in the afternoon, and criticize in the evening, has become a comrade and more through all seasons. My old friends in India, Shobha Aggarwal, Vrinda Grover, Amar Kanwar, and Myron Pereira, continue to inspire me by their activism. My brother, Depinder Singh, with whom I shared my childhood, has remained a loyal and steadfast companion on a journey begun together.

In the end, the biggest debt I owe is to my parents, Narinder Singh and Satinder Kapur, both activists in the teachers' movement in Delhi University, who gave me a sense of what living in a democratic socialist society is like. They practiced their politics in the way they ran our home and their friendships, making it forever strange to me that people's worth should be measured in terms of their market value.

Chapters 1, 3, 4, and 7 have been published in slightly modified forms and I wish to thank the following for permission to reprint them here: "Children Out of Control: The Debate on Children and Television in Late Twentieth Century America." In *Kids Media Culture*, ed. Marsha Kinder. Durham, N.C., and London: Duke University Press, 1999, 122–138. "Obsolescence and Other Playroom Anxieties." *Rethinking Marxism*, Volume 17, Number 2, April 2005, 239–257. "Free Market/Branded Imagination: Harry Potter and the Commercialization of

Children's Culture." *Jump Cut*, No. 46, Summer 2003. "The Postmodern Condition and Childhood's End: Hollywood's History Lessons for Children in the 1990s." *Film & History: An Interdisciplinary Journal of Film and Television Studies*, 2002, CD-ROM Annual.

Coining for Capital

Introduction

Without Training Wheels: The Ride into Another Century of Capital

Mr. and Mrs. Dursley, of number four, Privet Drive, were proud to say that they were perfectly normal, thank you very much. They were the last people you'd expect to be involved in anything strange or mysterious, because they just didn't hold with such nonsense.

—J. K. Rowling, *Harry Potter and the Sorcerer's Stone*

Mr. and Mrs. Dursley's nice and normal suburban bourgeois life is shattered the day they find their nephew, Harry Potter, on their doorstep. The day itself starts off ominously. A large tawny owl flutters by their window while they eat breakfast. On his way to work, Mr. Dursley spots a cat reading a map and people in cloaks gathered in bunches whispering the name Potter. Harry, now only a baby, will eventually turn out to be more powerful than the Dursleys. He is a wizard who will soon discover his ability to live by magic, while his aunt and uncle will remain routine-bound "Muggles" who want their lives to go on unchanged. Here we have a tale that speaks of a fear (and a hope) that is at least as old as the notion of childhood, which historians tell us became solidified only in the eighteenth century—that our children will turn out to be strangers to us and live in a world distinctly different from ours. However, Harry Potter also turned out to be a brand name that spearheaded a marketing campaign that sold not only the series of books but also films, video games, toys, and a horde of other commodities for both children and adults. In the global market of the end of the twentieth century, the magic of the Harry Potter story was turned into a means to serve the Mugglish ends of profit making.

The title of this book, *Coining for Capital*, is paraphrased from Karl Marx's passionate advocacy for shortening the working day for children younger than twelve. This law, Marx wrote, would prevent to some extent "the coining of children's blood into capital."[1] Marx spoke much of the widespread transformation of people—peasants, craftspeople, men, women, and children—into instruments of labor by industrial capital. A century and a half later, we are witnessing the full consequences of another aspect of the colonization of human life toward producing capital, that is, the production of people as consumers. I would like to open this book by pointing to a series of contradictions with which we as a society are confronting the idea of childhood today. An unprecedented number of commodities that line our market shelves evoke the idea of childhood while social protections to children and their families are withdrawn. While new fads hit the market every day that promise adults they can remain forever young, children are represented in popular culture, law, and public policy as little adults. Instead of imagining childhood as the birthplace of new possibilities, we are now confronting the death of the notion of childhood itself. Evidence of this death lies in the new image of children that has emerged in contemporary children's consumer culture, at the heart of which is the children's or family film. Quite simply, Hollywood's children have grown up, learning to live and manage by their wits in a world peopled by ineffective adults. These new children parody nineteenth-century notions that childhood is some special, eternal, pure state and children the opposite of adults.

Instead, they flaunt the blurring of boundaries between adulthood and childhood, bringing themes that were once the preserve of the horror or sci-fi genre into the children's film. When the toys in the *Toy Story* series (1995, 1999) come to life, they evoke neither wonder nor horror. Rather, much to our amusement, these postmodern toys talk anxiously about their brand identities and the companies that sell them. *Matilda* (1996) continues the trend of the *Home Alone* series (1990, 1992, 1997) by showing a child who quite literally raises herself, including finding herself a guardian, while her parents feverishly pursue money and the things it can buy. In *Jumanji* (1996), the children raise not only themselves but also the adults. In both *Jumanji* and *Jack*

(1996), childhood and adulthood are permeable and reversible; children can turn into adults and then back into children again.

In fact, Hollywood has taken enthusiastically to postmodern irony, telling us that childhood is merely a socially produced idea, a discursive phenomenon. Flattering us for our savvy knowledge that cinematic images are ideological constructions, it parodies earlier images of childhood, asking that we not take its representations "too seriously." Meanwhile, it continues, quite seriously, to develop mechanisms to increase and predict box-office receipts. In Arnold Schwarzenegger's *Last Action Hero* (1993), Danny, the fatherless child, challenges his adult hero, Jack, to speak out loud a word he has written on a piece of paper. When Jack is unable to do so, Danny, showing off his postmodern cool, crows: "You can't. You can't possibly say it! Because this movie is PG–13." While making fun of the concept of children's innocence that underlies the PG–13 film, the filmmaker has successfully made another PG–13 film. Irony here is the sugar coating that makes social conformism palatable. After all, a transformation as profound as the end of childhood and with it the hope of an alternative world does not go uncontested.

We can be fairly sure that a social transformation is well on its way when it makes its appearance in the children's or the family film. Packaged for bourgeois consumption, it is the most conservative of genres. Unlike sci-fi or horror, it attempts to reassure rather than alarm and to socialize children rather than paint extreme scenarios for adult consumption. Moreover, it casts the widest possible net for its audience. According to a survey by David Davis of Paul Kagan Associates that covered the years 1984–1991, PG-rated films were twice as likely as R-rated films to earn $60 million at the box office, and three times as likely to earn $100 million.[2] An industry committed to generating profits is not likely to risk subverting such a dependable source of revenue. Therefore, we would be overestimating Hollywood's creativity and influence if we ascribed the change in childhood to the images coming out of the family film, which, as Robert Allen has argued in "Home Alone Together," is the industry's response to the changing nature of both the family and film viewing. Allen traces the family film to the 1980s and 1990s, when Hollywood expected to generate profits from both the new demographic of an increasingly young audience and the market in video rentals and sales. Allen cites *Home Alone* as a leading film in this category. It made a killing in the theaters and the video market and also played out the altered family configuration in which a child whose parents are absent learns to depend upon himself. The point is that Hollywood is responding to and helping reinforce the reinvention of childhood by acting out the transformation, the reasons for which are both historical and economic.

The growing up of children extends well beyond the screens of U.S. movies. Children dress and behave like adults and have access to most of the same media, including television and the Internet. Anne Higonnet, analyzing recent images of childhood—including the work of photographer Sally Mann and commercials for the Calvin Klein fashion line—has shown in *Pictures of Innocence* that the sexually knowing child is replacing the romantic child in both avant-garde and commercial art.

The Blurring of Adulthood and Childhood

The growing up of children is not only a cultural image but a matter of law and social policy. Since the 1980s, certain fundamental institutions that had established childhood as a separate category from adults—juvenile delinquency laws, public assistance to poor families with children, public education—are being overturned. For instance, there is an increasing demand to reverse the protections of juvenile delinquency law and try children as adults if they are charged with murder or sexual assault. What had seemed the outlandish fantasy of a deranged mind in the 1950 horror film *The Bad Seed* is no longer a far-fetched idea. In the film, the mentally retarded gardener scares the "evil" child protagonist—itself a perverse idea then—by telling her that there are little electric chairs for children like her: a pink one for girls and a blue one for boys. Jeffrey Fagan and Valerie West indicate that the last time the Supreme Court considered the constitutionality of the death penalty for juveniles was in 1989 in *Stanford vs. Kentucky* (492 US 361, 1989), when it concluded that the death penalty was not disproportionate to the culpability of adolescents and that individualized assessments could adequately sort out which adolescents were sufficiently morally culpable. They argue that since 1994 when death sentences for juveniles peaked there has been a marked decline in death sentences for juveniles and an evolving trend that considers the death penalty cruel and unusual punishment for adolescents. However, the United States remains one of three nations, along with Iran and the Congo, where the death penalty is applied to those under eighteen.

Since the eighties, there has emerged a consensus at the top, among both Democrats and Republicans, that social welfare is an anachronism and families should take care of themselves and their children without social support. Howard Zinn recounts that between 1980 and 1984, President Reagan cut social services by $140 billion while increasing military expenditures by $181 million and cutting taxes by $190 billion (most of which went to the wealthy).[3] Welfare programs were cut, such as benefits to single mothers through the Aid to Families and Dependent Children Program, food stamps, and health care for the poor through Medicaid, and Social Security payments became regressive, that is, those lower on the economic ladder paid more. As unemployment grew during these years, so did the infant death rate. President Clinton's welfare reform bill (1996) further undercut government assistance to families: It limited public assistance to five years and included a provision that there would be no increase in state assistance with the birth of a new child.

This trend has continued under President George W. Bush, whose tax cuts and cuts in education and other social services have further hampered families and schools in taking care of children. The fiscal budget for the year 2003, $310 billion, represented, according to Jodi Edelstein, the greatest increase in military spending in the last twenty years and exceeded the combined military budgets of the next ten military powers.[4] The increased military spending and the tax cuts, 52 percent of whose benefits go to the richest 1 percent of Americans, were subsidized by cutting welfare programs that either directly impacted children, such as the children's health insurance program known as the State Children's Health Insurance Program and a children's vaccine program that took a cut of 18 percent, or their families, such as the Low Income Home Energy Assistance and Dislocated Workers Assistance programs.

Besides the family, the other wall that came between children and the market was the school and the accompanying notion of universal education. However, it was not until 1954, after the *Brown vs. Board of Education* judgment by the Supreme Court, that schools started being desegregated. Yet school neighborhoods continued to be segregated by class and race, aided by two Supreme Court decisions in the seventies (*San Antonio Independent School District vs. Rodrigues* and *Milken vs. Bradley*). Here the Court ruled that there would be no need to equalize funds between rich and poor school districts or to bus children from wealthy suburbs to the inner cities.[5] Moreover, the continued impoverishment of public education and its privatization through the voucher system betray the promise of universal education: that all children are entitled to a good education right in their neighborhood.

Increasingly, schools are imagined not as an alternative to the workplace but as miniversions of it. In the summer of 1998, I worked as a video teacher with the Mayor's Employment and Training Program, Chicago. Low-income young people were paid to take the various educational programs offered by the mayor's office as a substitute for school. However, at the orientation we were told that the name of the program had been changed to the Mayor's Workforce Development Summer Jobs Program. We were asked to think of the summer program not as a substitute for school but as a *job* for the students. Regardless of our area (English, math, or video production), we had to teach certain skills, such as writing resumes, dressing appropriately, filling out time sheets, and showing up on time. This is an open admission that schools cannot extend the childhood of working-class children and corroborates Ray Rist's thesis in *The Urban School* that the urban ghetto school functions as a "factory for failure" that fits its students for the same level in the labor market as their parents.

The cornerstone of free-market theory is that social welfare is an unfair intervention and a tax on free enterprise, and that the family should work and produce for itself—failing which, each individual should take on that task—rather than rely on social services. The paradox of free-market theory, whose costs are paid ultimately by the most vulnerable, including children, is that the family in the United States today is called upon to take care of children when its capability to do so is being systematically eroded. Stephen Resnick and Richard Wolff point to a number of factors that threw middle- and working-class families into crisis in the Reagan-Bush years. First, beginning in the seventies there was a fall in real income. Second, wages were further driven down as unions came to the bargaining table under the "new reality" of their members' taking lower-paid jobs or facing unemployment. Third, corporations came to labor negotiations strengthened by international trade agreements and innovations in finance and new technologies that enabled them to simply shut down a plant and move it to a third-world country where labor was cheaper. There was no state expenditure to offset these pressures. Instead, welfare programs were cut and Social Security taxes raised. Families met this crisis by going into debt just when interest rates on consumer debt increased, thus pulling families further into debt.[6]

Faced with the failure of the family to provide care, free-market theory takes the next logical step: It demands that individuals be responsible for themselves. When children are recognized as persons within this theory, autonomy and freedom mean that they are now free to experience the exploitation of the market. In a children's book from 1980, *Another Mouse to Feed*, the author, Robert Kraus, prepared children to live with Reaganomics. The story featured a family of mice in which the two parents worked several jobs to provide for their thirty-two children. (One of the tenets supporting the withdrawal of welfare was that the poor were responsible for their condition because of the "culture" of poverty, one of whose elements was that they just had too many children.)[7] One day, the children decided to help their parents. Those who went to school took on after-school jobs like cleaning cars, polishing shoes, and delivering pizza and groceries, while the eldest, "modeling himself after his father got two after-school jobs: delivering newspapers and sweeping up in a grocery store." Those too young to go to school did the housework and looked after the young ones, and "the money was soon rolling in." The "happy" end of the story was this: "Before long, Baby Mouse was helping too," as a cashier in a florist's shop. Here we have a return to childhood that resembles the sweatshops of nineteenth-century Manchester capitalism, when in opposition to the advocates against child labor the capitalists argued that children's little hands were particularly suited to certain forms of labor.[8]

Experts on childhood too now seem cavalier about children having to shoulder the burden of their own care. Some have begun to refer to children taking care of themselves—the "home alone" kids of lighthearted Hollywood comedies—as children in "self-care." Joe L. Kincheloe, who related the film *Home Alone* to contemporary children's experiences, called Kevin, the film's protagonist, "the self-sufficient, boy-hero of the postmodern era" and the film "a marketing bonanza."[9] This is how children are welcomed into the new century: Just like everyone else, they have to labor and produce for themselves. For all the wealth it generates, free-market society has no patience with those who can't pay for the ride—the sick, the elderly, the disabled, the children. At the same time, it continues to drive down the number who would have access to its sources with, as Zinn tells us, the top 1 percent of the nation owning one-third of it.[10]

While children's access to health, education, and care has increasingly become a chimera, market shelves are spilling over with children's things available for anyone who can pay the price. By the 1990s, the number of products for children—ranging from tangible ones such as toys, candy, cereal, snacks, carbonated and noncarbonated drinks, clothes, shoes, and books, to those for entertainment, such as films and videos, computer games, and entertainment parks—has far exceeded any other time in history. Children's marketers, echoing the demand that children be tried as adults by the judicial system, claim that children are a market just like another.

However, just because children no longer embody childhood does not mean that childhood itself has ended. Increasingly, childhood is evoked in all kinds of commodities sold to adults. The dissatisfactions of adulthood can now be dulled through the consumption of commodities. A recent television commercial for Nissan takes place in Toyland instead of on the usual slick rainy streets. An Indiana Jones type drives his sports car through toys and picks up a Barbie, leaving a Ken to wonder what happened to his tennis partner. Similarly, an ad for Cadillac carries a sepia-toned image of a young boy taking his first bicycle ride out of the arms of this father. The copy reads: "The last time you felt this exuberant, your dad let go." The ad does not address the consumer as a rational adult man who will make a carefully considered choice but as an adult whose inner child is waiting to be released. The car is just another toy for this big boy.

The market is an equal-opportunity granter of eternal youth to big girls as well, so long as they can pay the price. So we have Sears, a large retail chain, selling Winnie the Pooh bags and watches for adult women; Qualcom advertising a wireless phone by showing a Barbie look-alike using it, as if to suggest that childlike spontaneity can be found in the midst of climbing the career ladder; and, of course, that old drain on women's resources, cosmetics. Adult men and women are both sold objects whose final promise is not a phone or a lotion, but youth.

The Reinvention of Childhood and the Family

I argue that the end of childhood is not a media effect—the result of children seeing too much sex and violence—or an isolated effect of family dysfunction. Rather, it is inextricably connected to the wider historical and material changes in which children are increasingly imagined in culture and social policy, sold to in the market, and tried in judicial courts as adults. The change in the meaning of childhood is a structural feature of postmodernity, which, along with David Harvey and Fredric Jameson, I understand as the cultural logic of late twentieth-century capitalism.[11] It is an outcome of the shift from a Fordist to a post-Fordist mode of production, the dramatic growth of the United States as a consumer society, the development of a multinational global economy, new technologies, and the collapse of the traditional wage-earning-father family of the fifties, which, as Stephanie Coontz has brilliantly shown in *The Way We Never Were*, was in any case partly mythical. This study is located in the United States, where restraints on capital were systematically eroded in the last two decades of the twentieth century as it emerged as the world's most advanced consumer society. So what we are observing here is the extreme end of a phenomenon—one that is mitigated by law, social policy, and culture in other advanced capitalist countries, such as in Europe and Japan, or that occurs quite differently in the third world, where children are transformed into instruments of labor for a global market.[12]

My approach is Marxist feminist, which, I believe, provides a vantage point from which we can understand not only why we are confronting a new image of the child but also how to intervene and act upon this change. It is Marxist because I understand capitalism to be the overarching reality of our time, whose logic of turning every arena of our lives into an opportunity to accumulate capital has not spared any entity, including childhood. It is feminist because the history of childhood is inextricably interconnected with the family: with its invention as a private space in opposition to the public sphere of the market in industrial capitalism; with the relations between men and women as they developed within this idealized family; and with the labor of child care as divided between men and women. The changed relationship between children and adults represented in contemporary children's texts and films, I argue, is a cultural shift based on the transformation of the family in late capitalism.

Theorizing the relationship between the family and capitalism has been central to the socialist-feminist project, and its insights are invaluable to understanding the redefinition of childhood that is currently under way. How women's work in the home reproduced capital was the focus of a raging debate in the midseventies whose significance was that, first, it politicized the personal by putting housework on the political agenda, showing that it had economic value and was not simply a gift from women to men; and second, it showed that women's labor was instrumental in sustaining capital.[13] The work women did in the house, it was argued, took care of the emotional and physical needs of the male wage earner, making it possible for him to function in the harsh competitive relations of the market.

This family, termed "anti-social" by Michelle Barrett and Mary McIntosh or the "private family" by Coontz, was a pact between capital and patriarchy.[14] It made the market bearable for the male wage-earning worker by placing the labor and sexuality of women at his service within the home. As the home became the sole focus of women's labor and creativity, women were socialized into accepting this role through the cult of domesticity, which raised being wife and mother to the level of a sacred duty.

Children were placed at the heart of this family. In fact, children were given as the reason for its existence. The romanticizing of the child as the Other of the adult has the same foundations as the casting of woman as the Other of man. For instance, Jean-Jacques Rousseau argued through his fictional account *Emile* that any ordinary boy with the right education could be transformed into a citizen, thus making the assertion that all (men) were equal. While Rousseau was influential in presenting boys as pure points of origin innocent of sex, violence, and commerce, he considered girls unfit for education and citizenship because they were, according to him, by nature nurturing, rather than rationally thinking, beings.

In recent U.S. history, the family that approximated the nineteenth-century antisocial ideal was the suburban family of the post–World War II economic boom. This inward-looking nuclear family, a product of the nuclear threat and the cold war, Elaine Tyler May has shown in *Homeward Bound*, was sustained by women's labor and creativity, which was withdrawn from the public sphere and placed at the service of housework and child care. The socialist-feminist analysis of the bourgeois family as a pact between capital and patriarchy came from a generation of women raised by these fifties mothers and therefore intimately aware of its claustrophobia. Radicalized in the left movement, they tore apart the mystification of the home as an enclave safe from capital. They showed that instead the family was well integrated into capital: It served as the site of consumption when production shifted from the home to the factory. It followed then that the struggle to end exploitation—that is, living off another's labor—would begin at home, right where men owned and controlled women's labor and sexuality. The fundamental socialist-feminist insight was that capital needed the family to reproduce the worker, private property, and class. It also followed then that capital would not destroy the family.

Barbara Ehrenreich, writing from the vantage point of the eighties, comments in "Life without Father" on how that prognosis just didn't stand up to the test of history. Men, she argues, have shown no particular interest in upholding the patriarchal side of the bargain and have increasingly abdicated their traditional roles as the husbands, breadwinners, and petty patriarchs of the capitalism-plus-patriarchy paradigm. Neither has capital in its most ruthless form, the free market, shown any particular interest in maintaining the traditional family, as we can see from the antifamily policies of the New Right since the eighties, in spite of a heightened moral panic over the collapse of the family. Reporting on the changes in the family, Arlie Hochschild establishes the following: While in 1950 less than a fifth of the mothers with children worked in the labor force, that number has risen to two-thirds of all such households, with their salaries vital to the family budget by the year 2000. In addition, work is taking up increasing numbers of hours in the day, with middle-class U.S. couples adding three forty-hour weeks of work a year between 1989 and 1998. The U.S. divorce rate has increased to 50 percent, with one-fifth of the households with children headed by a single parent.[15]

In fact, feminism, particularly in its bourgeois form, Hochschild has argued, actually ended up collaborating with capital in breaking up the traditional family. As women have taken on careers, they have adopted the ethic of the market rather than humanizing it. Increasingly, she argues, housework, including care for children and the elderly, is institutionalized, commercialized, and sublet out of the home. Confronted by diminished social services and community, bourgeois women have come to depend upon the labor of working-class and third-world women for housework and child care, while those on the lower rungs of the economy are thrown into poverty.

Consequently, the spirit of domestic life too has been commercialized, including the way we talk about love. In contrast to Hochschild, Anthony Giddens in *The Transformation of Intimacy* welcomed the contractual relationship, suggesting that relationships between parents and children and between adult lovers should be based on a mutually satisfying contract rather than on economic need. Now, one of the achievements of feminism was that it demystified the language of love that had valorized the traditional household, showing that it was founded upon the oppression of women and children and the exploitation of women's labor and sexuality. So a mutually satisfying contract is certainly preferable to traditional models of authoritarian relationships. Yet is the exchange-based language of the market the only alternative to mystified sentimentality and the authoritarian relationships that it supports? How, for example, can care and love be written and quantified into a contract between individuals who have differential power and needs, particularly children and adults? Contractual language tends to homogenize all relationships, while we expect to connect differently in our relationships as parents, lovers, teachers, patients, children, or citizens. For instance, we have a different set of expectations for our local K-Mart than for our children.

The contemporary U.S. family is indeed varied and complex and economic need no longer the only motive that holds adults in a household together.[16] Children are now raised in households with a single adult and by step-parents and gay couples, and they move between parental households. These varied households indicate the possibilities of constructing consensual egalitarian relationships within households.

However, the disintegration of the family, premised upon new technologies and capitalist expansion, has brought its members face-to-face with the market. First, the shift to a flexible mode of production has made the home once again a place of production for the market. Second, the last of those in enclaves protected from capital—bourgeois children—are now invited to enter the market as consumers, with the family no longer standing as a protective wall between them and the market. New technologies such as laptops, pagers, cellular phones, additional telephone lines, email, and the Internet have created at one extreme "corporate soldiers," the highly paid multinational executives who take their laptops and fax machines even on a vacation, and at the other extreme the army of underpaid, temporary, work-intensive, home-based computer professionals entering data or running computer programs for corporations. New middle-class houses are now sold with home-office rooms, and large stores like Office Depot and Staples sell largely to small businesses run out of the home. Numerous articles in popular parenting magazines describe "stressed-out families," that is, families with little private or leisure time. Frequent advice from *Parents* magazine, for example, is to restore the traditional separation of home and work by shutting off the fax machine, screening phone calls, letting the answering machine take the calls, and so on, so adults can be at "home" with the family.

In some cases, the capital and patriarchy pact is invoked yet again to keep the home the private responsibility of women while using women's labor, still cheaper than men's, to generate profits. Or alternatively, jobs done by women are characterized as low skilled. In *Women's Employment and Multinationals*, Ruth Pearson and Diana Elson described how young Moroccan women who were previously considered illiterate were being taught to assemble computers based on their sewing skills. This ploy saved the costs of training these women more completely and also justified their low wages. Similarly, Annie Phizacklea and Carol Wolkowitz show in *Homeworking Women* that home-based women workers are obliged to take low-paid, insecure jobs that perpetuate their status as holding primary responsibility for children and domestic work.

This is, of course, not shown in commercials for new technologies. One television commercial for MCI, for instance, shows a woman madly working at her home office via the phone, the modem, the fax machine, and email to drive hard bargains with men in traditional offices. She is, however, in her pajamas and bunny slippers. In another commercial, this one for Advanced Micro Devices, a mother looks at a computer screen with a placid baby sleeping in her arms. These happy scenarios of women who "have it all" are made possible, Arlie Hochschild has shown, through the exploitation of the labor of third-world and working-class women to whom domestic work, including child care and the care of the elderly, is outsourced.[17]

In its post-Fordist avatar, we are seeing capitalism push the workday way beyond what Marx imagined, but it follows a logic that he identified as central to capitalism: In its incessant drive to maximize profit, capital "oversteps not only the moral, but even the merely physical maximum bounds of the working-day."[18] We see this reflected in advertisements for products and services that guarantee that nothing can stop us from working. A United Airlines print advertisement makes a joke of the end of leisure by claiming: "We fly to Latin America's most desirable destinations, according to your boss." An advertisement by Verizon shows a woman waiting in what appears to be an airport lounge. She has her laptop in front of her and holds up a V sign. The copy reads: "Now pack your minutes with every business trip." When business goes on around the clock, seamlessly connecting labor and markets in different time zones, time, reduced to its minutest fraction, seems to be endlessly running out.

As capitalism has expanded, it has broken down the barricades of the "antisocial" family to socialize it into capitalist relations. Our response has to be a "family" that is varied and dynamic, socialized into a society where individuals find self-realization with others and not in isolation. To a certain extent, the bourgeois family provided a space to try out relations not allowed by the market, where, as Walter Benjamin suggested, those antagonistic to the present could live by codes they strived for in the future.[19] The goal, however, is to end the antagonism of public and private, for while the privatized family may provide for some a brief escape from a hostile world, it ultimately allows that world to continue unchanged.

The argument that runs through this book is that the new image of the child sits at the intersection of capitalist expansion and new technologies, both of which have enabled the child to grow up. New technologies have enabled children to have access to the world and increased their abilities to a degree unprecedented in history, making it possible for children literally to take care of themselves. Capitalist expansion has turned children into little adults making consumer choices if they have the money and fending for themselves if they don't, alone and isolated, vulnerable to abuse in both the family and the market. New technologies open up the possibilities of integrating children into society and in turn creating a society that, because it nurtures children, nurtures all its members. Imagine a society where tales of children's fear of being abandoned by parents in a hostile world are recounted as historical tales from a distant past.

In a remarkable passage in "Capital, Volume I," Marx writes about the potential of modern industry to integrate children into adult life:

> However terrible and disgusting the dissolution, under the capitalist system, of the old family ties may appear, nevertheless, modern industry, by assigning as it does an important part in the process of production, outside the domestic sphere, to women, to young persons, to children of both sexes, *creates a new economic foundation for a higher form of the family, and of the relations between the sexes. . . . Moreover, it is obvious that the fact of the collective working group being composed of individuals of both sexes and all ages, must necessarily, under suitable conditions, become a source of humane*

development; although in its spontaneously developed brutal, capitalistic form, where the labourer exists for the process of production, and not the process of production for the labourer, that fact is a pestiferous source of corruption and slavery.[20] [Emphasis mine].

Looking at our world from the vantage point of childhood reveals the dialectical nature of capital itself. For childhood was both a product of and a protest against capital. It was the overall increase in material abundance generated by new technologies and collective labor that made it possible to sustain the idea that children should be freed from the responsibility of labor and instead spend their childhood playing and learning. Childhood, one of the promises to emerge from social labor, was imagined as the exact opposite of alienated labor. As opposed to the constraints of alienated labor, children's play could be driven by curiosity, the need to explore all of one's abilities for its own sake (just as children climb a tree over and over again to perfect their climbing), and a sensuous and tactile relationship with the world that had no market value. In reclaiming childhood, first as the right of children and then for us all, we can find a goal to guide our politics now. Quite simply, it means putting children first and unwaveringly committing ourselves to the idea that all the world's children are our children.

On a Personal Note

This book started out as a way of understanding a children's culture that my two young children—Suhaila, who was then six, and Nilim, barely two—were entering. Late twentieth-century North American children's culture, I felt, had little in common with my own growing up in India in the sixties. Suhaila and Nilim were incessantly teaching me about a children's consumer culture—toys, movie promotions, video games, stories, and characters—that I did not recognize from my own childhood. Cleaning up the children's room, I would try to remember the toys I had played with and could recall only a few board games I had shared with my brother.

Yet I soon found out that this children's consumer culture befuddled even parents who had grown up in the United States. Of course, Suhaila's friends' parents could remember the television character Lamb Chop from their childhood days, while to Suhaila's deep astonishment I first saw television when I was eleven. Yet we were all new to computer and video games and the new fads that hit the children's market every other day. Even more significant, there were few concrete traces left of our childhood homes and neighborhoods. The world we knew as children was rapidly disappearing, while we come to the present as latecomers, compelled to unlearn old knowledge while learning the new along with our children, like first-generation immigrants who learn to navigate the new landscape and speak the language through their children born there.

The incomprehension with which we as a generation face our children's lives is, I believe, directly connected to our feelings of inadequacy in understanding and therefore exercising some control over the world that we live in. Confronted by a world whose economic system and technological power seem beyond our grasp, Fredric Jameson has suggested, leads to a paralysis of thought and action that supports the wild conspiracy theories that abound in the cultural imaginary these days in films such as *Matrix* (1999) or *The Truman Show* (1998).[21] Nothing occurs to a collective social imaginary that is unable to, and perhaps unwilling to, understand and act upon the world. Another aspect of such an imaginary is that it characterizes a stultified adult.

Jameson has related this "structure of feeling" to postmodernity, which he identifies as the cultural logic of late capitalism. Postmodernity in this view, to which I subscribe as well, does not imply the end of capital, only its radicalization. I make the argument in subsequent pages that what we are witnessing is not something drastically new but a radicalization of processes inherent in capitalist expansion, which through the incessant invention of new knowledge and technologies deconstructs essences and turns them into commodities. In these pages, I explore how children's consumer culture deconstructs childhood, transforming it from an essential attribute embodied by children into a commodity.

Therefore, we can find our experiences at the turn of the twenty-first century echoed by Walter Benjamin's from half a century ago. Writing of the difficulties of holding on to childhood memories in the face of the quickly changing urban landscape of Berlin in the 1930s, he described them as "evanescent and as alluringly tormenting as half forgotten dreams."[22] My grandmother's life, thanks to imperialist subdivisions of Asia and Africa, spanned the birth of three countries. Born in Burma, she grew up in Pakistan and came to India during the partition riots that accompanied Indian independence in 1947. A refugee two times, displaced from "homes" which became "foreign countries," she was half-disbelieving of the stories she told us about her own childhood, many of which she would have preferred to forget or, I am sure, censored for our ears. In turn, my brother and I could not imagine the village that was her childhood home, just as my children cannot see the modest middle-class New Delhi bungalow I grew up in, which has now been replaced by a three-storied structure with six apartments.

The disappearance of the world we knew as children, with only images left as evidence of that time—photographs and, where there are no photographs, personal memories—profoundly destroys the idea that childhood is some eternal, unchanging, fixed state. Displacement from our childhood—the sense that one's childhood is a "half-forgotten dream" with very little left of that time that we can show, teach, or see in our children's lives—is a fundamental feature of modernity that is even more radicalized at the turn of the twenty-first century. It is a feeling that comes over me when, even as I stand around with friends while our children eat ice cream that drips all over their clothes or walk with them to the corner store for candy, it seems that these quintessential images of childhood are intrinsically fragile—especially as elsewhere, both here and abroad, children's lives are under the constant threat of poverty and war.

The Book in Outline

My aim in this book is to answer two questions: What is the new image of childhood that is replacing the old? And what are the historical and material reasons for the transformation of childhood? To answer these, I have analyzed the public discourse about childhood in three interrelated phenomena: the invention of children as a niche market by marketing research following World War II, the political economy of the children's film as a part of children's consumer culture, and finally children's film texts from the last decade of the twentieth century. The combination of textual analysis of films and the political economy of the children's film as part of children's consumer culture is made necessary by the increasing integration of media industries in late twentieth-century capitalism such that no one text can be consumed in isolation.

I begin my analysis in Chapter 1 by examining the role played by television and children's marketing in constructing children as knowing consumers rather than innocent receivers of gifts. Television as a medium is central to the experience of postmodernity. It erodes the public/private boundary on which the home is based, directly addresses children over the heads of their parents, creates a global generation of children, and, as David Harvey shows, collapses time and space by bringing disparate images, both historical and geographical, simultaneously into the living room in a more or less uninterrupted flow.[23]

From Chapter 2 onward, I look at specific films to outline the contradictions and anxieties that abound around the reinvention of childhood, for a transformation as profound as this is deeply contested. While I am identifying a trend toward the redefinition of childhood, this trend is opposed and contradicted, often within the same text. I begin by looking at nostalgic attempts to hold on to a disappearing idea in the ways in which the girl child is imagined across three versions of A Little Princess: first, Frances Hodgson Burnett's book from the "golden age" of children's literature; second, the Shirley Temple film from 1940, a film from the "golden age" of the child star; and finally the nostalgia that characterizes its most recent version, made in 1995 by Alfonso Cuaron. Nostalgia, like childhood, is both regressive and progressive. It simultaneously expresses the longing for patriarchal and imperial control while it protests the commercialization of childhood.

In Chapter 3, I discuss Pocahontas and The Indian in the Cupboard, both produced in the quincentennial of Columbus's landing in America, and examine the ways in which the relationship of children, history, and utopia is reconceptualized in late capital and its implications for how childhood is imagined.

Following this, I analyze four films that, in my view, present a new image of childhood. These films redefine childhood by blurring the boundaries between adulthood and childhood, between the public and the private, and construct a new conception of children's relationship to time, commodities, play, and the imagination. The films I discuss are Toy Story (1995), Jumanji (1996), Matilda (1996), and Harry Potter (2002).

My strategy here is to pit the image of the child as it is being reinvented against the image from a century ago. Consequently, I juxtapose, quite eclectically, representations of childhood in children's books and films and the adult genres of horror and sci-fi from the earlier half of this century with images from contemporary children's films and consumer culture. The reason for doing so is to defamiliarize the present moment as one that is a cause for alarm but also for hope, if we can wrest childhood from the claws of capital.

In this struggle we should think of children as our collaborators. Just as we teach children to read and write, clothe and feed themselves, in a bid to make them autonomous members of society, we should teach them to think critically, organize, collaborate with others, and protest so that they can cope with a system that is essentially hostile to life and therefore to children. One response to the growing up of children has been to regain control over them through repressive "zero-tolerance" policies, as the young are forcibly pushed back into the mold of innocent childhood just when everything else is pushing them to grow up socially. This view is a mistaken one, turning us into cops who police our own children. However, it is not our children who are out of control but the free market, which is eroding every collective effort to make this world one where the most vulnerable among us can be safe.

1 | Cradle to Grave

*Children's Marketing
and the Deconstruction
of Childhood*

In a print advertisement for a wireless home network sold by Symphony, we see a family engaged in a tug-of-war over their single computer. "Stop the war, cut the cord," advises the copy, asking parents to buy the wireless service so as to have several connections at the same time and end the family tussles over access to the Internet. The choice of words is tongue-in-cheek, speaking of a new and changed family environment in which family peace is established by freeing children from parental control. The cord is not umbilical but technological and the child's autonomy achieved by buying another new market-produced commodity. This promise of independence, of course, is also at the root of the widespread alarm that new media technologies are stealing children away from the family, exposing them to adult secrets of sex, violence, and commerce, and destroying childhood.

One technical fix to this concern was the V-chip. In 1995 the U.S. Congress legislated that television sets should come equipped with a computer chip that would allow parents to block programming they considered unsuitable for their children. This is as logical as calling in the television repair person to fix the content on television, repeating a pattern in the battle with media makers that is by now well established. First, television broadcasters were freed from the demands to do something about what passes for children's television. Second, the costs of installing the V-chip were passed on to us, the consumers, as manufacturers built them into the price of television sets. Third, parents, particularly mothers, were once again enlisted as their children's enemy or drill sergeant, asked to carry out the orders of the experts to control children and protect them from television. Underlying the V-chip solution is the assumption that television is the main culprit in children's loss of innocence and that its power can be restrained by a reinstatement of parental authority.

One major impasse in the debate on children and television is that it has continued to be embedded within arguments centered on the "effects" of television on children. On one side are critics in the tradition of the Frankfurt school, such as Marie Winn, Neil Postman, and Steven Kline, who argue that television kills children's imaginations with limited colonizing narratives, violates their innocence in relation to sex, violence, and commerce, and, like a narcotic, numbs their innate curiosity about the world.[1] Basic to these claims is the assumption that children will mimic what they see—upon seeing violence, they will act violently.

On the other side, cultural studies has drawn attention to the varied ways in which audiences negotiate with, resist, or are co-opted by mass culture. Ellen Seiter and David Buckingham have emphasized that children do not inevitably absorb all the meanings and purposes of media content.[2] For instance, as Buckingham points out in his study of children's responses to television violence, although children may find certain scenes worrying or frightening, they develop ways of coping with them, such as changing channels, fast-forwarding, watching with others, and so on. The assertion here is that children are not cultural dupes, but discriminating and imaginative audiences.

Of course, no one disputes that children's television is filled with themes and narratives that reflect and reinforce the inequalities of race, gender, class, and sexuality. Rather, the difference between the two positions is that while the latter favors critical engagement with television, the former can lend itself to a ban on television viewing for children. However, the approaches are similar in that they have neglected the social history of childhood and assume childhood to be more or less a natural category simply discovered, and not invented, by television. This view leads to rehashing old arguments about the extent to which children's imaginations are co-opted by television (the same arguments were applied to comic books, cinema, and now the

Internet) and ignores the widespread social belief and experience that at the end of the twentieth century a fundamental transformation has occurred in the notion of childhood itself. When critics like Postman and Winn issue warnings about the "disappearance of childhood" (the title of Postman's book), they hold television to be the main culprit in the redefinition of childhood. Its accomplices in pulling children "out of the garden" (from the title of Steven Kline's book) are permissive parents who appear to have abandoned parenting to television.

Meanwhile, the loudest voices proclaiming that childhood is not an eternal, essential state but a constantly changing one, that children are, perhaps, only miniature adults, are children's marketers, who since the end of World War II have been inventing children as a new, hitherto undiscovered market. The impact of this campaign is now fully apparent. In contrast to the claim that television is corrupting children's innocence, these marketing men and women reiterate the opinion of Cy Schneider (a leading children's marketer whose credits include Barbie and Nickelodeon) that television is simply responding to the tastes of a generation of children that is not innocent like its predecessors: "Children are not that easy to entertain or persuade; they will not watch everything put in front of them on television, and will not buy (or ask to buy) everything that is cleverly advertised to them. In reality, children are intelligent, discriminating, and skeptical. Despite their lack of experience, they are not that easily fooled."[3] Similarly, another standard textbook on children's marketing, by Selina S. Guber and Jon Berry, stresses that the children of the present generation are "wise beyond their years": "Do you know what successful companies like Nike, Nabisco, Levi Strauss, McDonald's, Mattel, and Nintendo all have in common? The answer is that they have brilliantly tapped into the needs, interests, fantasies and desires of a huge, powerful, and growing consumer group—kids! Marketing studies show that today's new generation of wise-beyond-their-years children have gained unprecedented influence over family purchases—from clothes . . . to cars . . . to computers. It's a $120 billion market right now and the end is not yet in sight!" Even the Disney Corporation (which has built an empire on sentimentalized, fuzzy images of childhood innocence) announced in the midnineties: "It is no longer an innocent period of time." What is at stake in these statements is not a description of childhood but its invention, which is at the same time a deconstruction of the nineteenth-century model of the innocent child.[4]

Kid's Choice

The most significant change in the cultural notion of childhood in the last decades of the twentieth century was the construction of children as knowing consumers, overturning two hundred years of thinking of children as innocent receivers of gifts. Yet right from the eighteenth century, as historian J. H. Plumb suggests in *Birth of a Consumer Society*, childhood was both a commercial and a cultural category. Children were at the heart of the nuclear bourgeois family that became the dominant ideal in industrial capitalism. In the early stages of the industrial revolution, capitalism took production out of the household and family and collectivized it in the factory. Households stopped producing most of what they needed and bought it in the market. Production shifted to the factory, and the family became the site of consumption.

The nuclear family, as Michelle Barrett and Mary McIntosh have pointed out in *The Anti-social Family*, was produced at the intersection of patriarchy and capitalism. The bourgeois home or the "anti-social family" was constructed as the private sphere, where affection, security, intimacy, sexual love, and parenthood could be expressed and lived. This sanctuary stood in opposition to the alienated relations of the market that were based on exchange, temporariness, and disposability. Although it was not a product of capitalism, the family served as a key institution in the reproduction of capitalist ideology and social relations. It was the way of passing on private property and class membership, and it provided for the male wage earner a "home" or "haven" in the heartless world of the factory and the market, where human relations were governed by the logic of money and market value.

Children were at the core of the industrial family, for they were seen as providing the reason and justification for its existence. Humphrey Carpenter's and Jackie Wullschlager's studies of eighteenth- and nineteenth-century romantic literature show that the task of raising children was elevated to the level of sacred duty, and children were idealized as having a visionary and spiritual simplicity denied to adults.[5] Jean-Jacques Rousseau imagined children as the embodiment of eternal truth outside the contradictions of sexuality and social inequality. Imbuing the domestic sphere with a religious aura was a response to the secularization of the public sphere.

The glorification of children as innocent had real consequences for children. Bourgeois children had to be protected from what were characterized as adult secrets—money, sex, and social violence. Conversely, working-class children had to unlearn in school and special institutions their knowledge of these "facts of life." By the beginning of the twentieth century, according to Viviana Zelizer in *Pricing the Priceless Child*, U.S. children (including working-class children) were expelled from the market as labor. This was accompanied, Zelizer argues, by sentimentalizing children as objects of adult affection whose value could not be measured in terms of money. Money, like sex, was a taboo not to be discussed in front of children, who were at most allowed to play with token money while being showered with gifts.

Consequently, although the nineteenth century had a growing market for children in clothes, books, furniture, and toys, children were not sold to directly. Instead, they were imagined as untainted receivers of gifts. Gifts to children were considered expressions of parental love and therefore priceless. Imagine any of the characters of those classical Victorian stories—Peter Pan or Alice, for instance—looking for a good "deal." In her excellent study *The Case of Peter Pan*, Jacqueline Rose notes that James M. Barrie's book did not start out as made "for" children. Rather, its first appearance was as a novel for adults titled *The Little White Bird* (1902). Its transformation into a children's classic, Rose argues, was a function of the huge trade that targeted children's literature at adults that emerged in England at the turn of the century. At this early stage in the commercialization of children's culture, there was a certain embarrassment in profiting off childhood. The first edition of *Peter Pan*, Rose reports, came with an announcement on the first page indicating that proceeds from its sales would go to the children's hospital in London, Rose reports. Moreover, *Peter Pan* was marketed to adults, with the child ideally presented as the consumer. In much the same way that pet foods are sold these days to pet owners, the sales pitch promised adults that the book would make the child happy, obedient, and loving.

Childhood: The Final Frontier

The unrelenting pursuit of profit that drives capitalist expansion has shredded the last remnants of that embarrassment at profiting off childhood, as marketers have stopped worrying and started celebrating children as the largest and fastest-growing market segment. The invention of children as consumers is part of the larger logic of capitalist expansion after World War II, driven by the escalating development of the United States as a consumer economy while production shifted further to the third world. Since the sixties, technological and organizational changes have accelerated production, confronting businesses with lower rates of profit in the face of oversupply of commodities. The only solution to this problem endemic to capitalism is to drive down the cost of labor and to increase its productivity. It drives down costs by shifting production into the third world; hiring cheap labor, including children; and breaking laws and policies that protect labor. It increases productivity through technical innovations that speed up production and accelerate exchange and distribution systems.

David Harvey in *The Condition of Postmodernity* has characterized this change as the shift from the factory-centered Fordist mode of production to the flexible mode. In place of producing in a factory, labor is now spread across continents, outsourced or sublet to smaller and smaller units, including private homes. Digital technologies have made it possible to control production over geographically dispersed areas, while organizational changes have focused on small-batch production and stock-inventory reduction, thus reducing turnover time. For instance, a computer programmer in Hyderabad, India, can take over work at the exact point where his counterpart left off in Silicon Valley, while getting paid a sixth of the latter's salary. Electronic banking and plastic money are among the ways that have increased the speed with which commodities can be converted back into capital, and money can circulate and make more money.

This speeding up of production and exchange is matched by a tremendous growth in the production of consumer goods that include not only tangible products like shoes, clothes, cars, and bathrooms, but also services, particularly culture spectacles and entertainment. As David Harvey elaborates, while there are physical limits to the material goods that we can consume (even taking into account Imelda Marcos's famous six thousand pairs of shoes), there are virtually no limits to our ability to take in entertainment products like films, video games, and visits to theme parks. The shift to fashion or style from function or use is quite central to expanding the market. It makes people buy more of the same thing (we might not need shoes, but we'll buy a certain style that is currently in fashion), making obsolete what we already have.

The invention of children as a market and the rapid growth in children's consumer culture are logical outcomes of the expansion of the consumer economy in the affluent nations, reaching their pinnacle in the United States. Driving this expansion is market research, which underwent a major shift following World War II. Until the fifties, marketing research was sales oriented. It consisted of getting a product that had already been made to places where people would buy it. The consumer was a point at the end of the production line to be sold the item. Since the fifties, according to Robert Keith's standard text on marketing, "a Copernican revolution" has taken place: "The consumer became the sun" around which contemporary marketing strategy would evolve.[6] Market research now preceded the product, employing an increasing array of psychological methods to find an audience that would consume the planned product. This development, Eric Larson indicates, was motivated in the fifties by the intensified competition among advertisers for consumers in a saturated market, where a number of look-alikes competed with each other against the fear that people already had everything they needed.[7]

Marketing responded by focusing its attention on the consumer even more closely, beginning now to produce consumers before the product. Consumers were studied as ever-diminishing groups, defined as niche, regional, or even particle markets rather than as mass homogenized collections of people. This development was made possible, first, by innovations in research methods, including statistical and psychological approaches; and second, by developments in technologies that made it possible to tabulate large amounts of data via computers and keep records of consumer behavior via developments like scanner data. Scanner data give corporations the ability to track what we buy based on the information on our credit cards and grocery cards that are scanned each time we use them to make purchases. These market segments are constructions. Unlike class, gender, race, or sexuality, the categories are not based on historical and material relations of power. Instead, they present themselves as psychological or lifestyle markers under which everyone is hypothetically equal but different in what they desire.

We are by now familiar with marketing terms such as "yuppies," "empty-nesters," "style-setters," "generation Xers," "preteens," and so on to describe social groups. "The mass market is dead," Larson quotes Philip Kotler, according to whom the United States had entered the era of "mass customization in which computer technologies and automaton capabilities within factories now allow us to bring out affordable, individualized versions of products—every consumer's dreams."[8] Now let us be clear that this promise of abundance and every need filled is quite dependent on the ability of an individual to be a consumer, that is, to pay. There is nothing here about using these advanced methods of production, or prediction, and analysis to distribute social needs like housing, health, or education. All niche marketing does, in contrast to the earlier mass marketing, is further radicalize the production and surveillance of consumers by refining the tools of selling and the products to be sold. For all the talk about speaking to the individual, the intent behind niche marketing is to reaggregate our money toward generating profits for a diminishing number of corporations and similar products.

This is no "Copernican revolution" but simply a continuation of capital's need to accumulate capital. To convert investment into profit and therefore back into capital, the capitalist depends upon the consumer to buy. To entice people into buying or, in Marx's words, "lead the fly to the gluepot," capitalism considered "every real and possible need" a selling opportunity.[9] David Harvey, reading Marx, points out in *The Condition of Postmodernity* that the only way for capital to accumulate is to find an effective demand for a product, backed by the ability of the consumer to pay. If there is demand for a product but no capacity to pay for it, the capital invested in it fails to transform itself into profit and therefore, more capital. I am reminded of being lured into getting my daughter's pictures taken by a photo studio that advertised an affordable price for a portrait. However, once the photos were taken, we were invited to a showing of the varied images taken, whose prices were way beyond our budget. When we refused to buy them, the salesperson just dumped them into the wastebasket. There are worse accounts of capital's greed to maintain prices, including throwing grain into the sea rather than feeding the hungry during the depression years.

Other than at the site of production, capital is at its most vulnerable at the point of consumption. We cannot be forced to part with our money to consume, and that is why capitalism invests heavily in its core applied discipline, market research. The goal of market research, as Eric Larson points out, is to "capture, quantify, and distill the soul of the American consumer."[10] Tracking the lives and habits of consumers to the minutest extent acquired a greater degree of sophistication due to techniques such as scanner data and the ability of computers to organize large amounts of data. Eric Larson's *The Naked Consumer* is an incisive description of the development of marketing research from mass marketing to mass surveillance, from

targeting the masses to targeting masses of individuals. Both Larson
and Seiter have described the common experience of parents, one I
have gone through myself, who get unasked-for packages in the mail
that mark the developmental steps in a child's life. Mailers for diapers, baby food, and formula arrive with precision at the appropriate
time in the child's development. (Mine were generated from a ques-
tionnaire I naively filled in while waiting in the midwife's office, lured
by the promises of free samples and coupons that would help cut the
costs of having a baby while in graduate school.)

Children, like adults, have entered the lexicon of marketers as seg-
ments to be studied, targeted, and sold to corporations as commodities. For example, just as adults who subscribe to a magazine or apply
for a credit card get placed on lists that are shared and thus get junk
mail, children make it to these lists and are sold as commodities. In
Marketing to and through Kids, Selina Guber and Jon Berry advise po-
tential children's marketers that lists can be bought from Children's
Television Workshop (the Sesame Street folks), *Sports Illustrated for
Kids,* and *Parenting* magazine. Another list, the Young Family Index,
with 3.6 million households, offers about 85 percent coverage of all
births in the country. There are other direct-mailing lists that subdi-
vide families by the ages of their children and by ethnicity. Guber and
Berry give the example of Sears, which ran its list through databases
to find households with young children and then mailed them a cata-
log of back-to-school clothing. Probably the day one of my children
will get his or her own telemarketing call is not far away. My daughter already receives e-mails from Joann Fabrics and the American Girl
Store after entering her name for a lottery at the former and subscrib-
ing for a year to the latter's magazine.

Children have also joined the groups under surveillance for their
viewing and consuming patterns. The Neilsen group, the touchstone
for measuring ratings that drive advertising on television, include children over the age of two in their studies. The Neilsen people-meter, a
device that records who is watching television and when, assigns but-
tons to every family member over two years old. The youngest child
is assigned button number one on the remote control that is used to
turn on the television. The children, like the adults, are expected to
keep a record of their viewing by pressing the same button to start
the set and then remembering to press it again when they stop watching. The people-meter was met with strong protests by minority groups
when it was reintroduced in 2004, on the grounds that it seriously

underrepresented the viewing habits of minority audiences. Its consequences would be fewer minority-based programs and reduced work for minority artists. That is why we say that "money talks." Recognition as a consumer, not as a citizen, is the basis for being heard in a capitalist democracy.

The importance of the Neilsen ratings in determining what gets on television bears out Dallas Smythe's insight that commercial television produces audiences as commodities to be sold to corporations. Smythe claims in "Communications" that when we watch television, we are in reality working for capital; television executives make profits by selling advertising space to marketers by promising them an audience for their commercials. In other words, our leisure time is also appropriated toward accumulating capital, as television executives deliver us as commodities to marketing executives. Arguing that the raison d'être for television was to advertise market-produced commodities, Smythe equated television programming (other than commercials) with free lunches served in taverns in the 1900s to lure customers to buy beer.

Eileen Meehan further clarified this position in "Commodity Audience," highlighting that it was not simply by watching television but through the ratings system that audiences were produced as commodities. It was the rating system that provided the measure by which different prices were paid for programs based upon the number of people watching them. Claiming that children are no different from adults from the point of view of commercial television, Schneider reminds his critics that "commercial television's first mission is to entice viewers to watch the commercials. If commercial television cannot move goods, it cannot remain in business. Just because commercial television devotes many of its hours to the special audience of children doesn't change this fundamental point of view one iota."[11]

Some of the most cutting-edge innovations in marketing research have been in the area of children's marketing. Leaving aside the limitations of empirical research that can make a record only of what a person buys, marketers are now turning to anthropology, cultural studies, semiotics, socialization and cognitive development, and other humanistic approaches to understand all aspects of human behavior in the shopping arena. Even Marx, that astute critic of capitalism, has begun to be studied in marketing research. Elizabeth Hirschman and Morris Holbrook encouragingly advance the idea that once "one tames one's preconceptions and steps back from the political arena, basic

Marxist philosophy appears neither especially disturbing nor even counterintuitive."[12] Market research is now openly conceding what Marxist-driven cultural studies critics have condemned as the consequences of consumer culture—the feelings of envy, insecurity, and isolation—and putting them to use in further selling commodities.

Ethnography, another critical tradition that has a history of resistance to capitalist exploitation of nature and human societies, is likewise being pressed into the service of market research. According to McNeal in *Kids as Customers*, ethnographic observation is a particularly useful tool in understanding children's behavior in stores, to get hold of "youth specific jargon" for use in advertising and to decide where to place products. Guber and Barry in *Marketing to and through Kids* give the example of Levi-Strauss, who got parents' permission to follow their kids on their shopping trips and also to look inside their children's closets before coming up with its "wild creatures" campaign aimed at kids. Drama and role playing are cited as other favorite techniques.

Niche marketing makes visible all the senseless wastefulness of capitalism. Marketers compete over an increasingly smaller market, spend billions of dollars on making similar products look different (e.g., differentiating one chocolate cereal from another), and inventing new products. The vast majority of new products are spin-offs of television and film themes and characters. There are also straightforward replications of adult products for children with essentially no difference between the two other than the packaging. For instance, children's toothpaste hit the market in the mideighties with Aquafresh for Kids. It was soon followed by Crest for Kids and Colgate Jr., and now it seems that every new film comes with a toothpaste, shampoo, and conditioner. Sony and Fischer-Price have come up with electronics (tape recorders, camcorders) that are marketed to kids. This "diversification" of the market rises to further levels of absurdity when adult products already downscaled for children are further miniaturized. Take your pick from this mind-numbing variety—Bite Size Chips Deluxe, Bite Size Rainbow Chips Deluxe, Bite Size Pecan Sandies, Mini Middles, Clubette crackers, Sweet Spots shortbread cookies, and Elfkins sandwich cookies. Little wonder that the ethnographer carefully observing people in a grocery store gleefully reported to Larson that shoppers are in such a trancelike state that they are unaware of being under surveillance.[13]

A large number of multinational corporations now make goods for children on an international basis and are household names in the

United States—General Foods, General Mills, Quaker, and Ralston; Mattel, Hasbro, Fischer-Price, LEGO, Nintendo, and Coleco; Hershey's, Mars M&Ms, and Nabisco; American Greetings and Hallmark; Walt Disney, Hanna-Barbera, and Warner Communications; Burger King and McDonald's. While children's consumer culture dates back to the fifties, the eighties saw an explosion. This ranged across children's media—cable networks (such as Nickelodeon and Cartoon Network), magazines (*Sports Illustrated for Kids*), and newspapers (*Young American*). Children were organized as clubs (Burger King Kid's Club, Fox Kid's Club) to initiate them into junk-mail culture.

The niche market for children is the site of a battle to win children to brands as early as possible. There are, for example, children's clothing (GapKids), books (WaldenKids), banking (First Children's Bank), and hospitality (Camp Hyatt). The "battle" is defined by Gene Del Vecchio, a children's marketer: "At stake is a portion of more than a $160 billion pie. But it is not size or resources that will win it, for small brands can and do become massive overnight. The battle will be won by the company that best understands kids, their emotional needs, their fantasies, their dreams, their desires. Such knowledge is the mightiest weapon in a marketer's arsenal to win a child's heart."[14]

The $160 billion figure varies across estimates; David Leonhardt and Kathleen Kerwin estimated that in 1998, kids under fourteen spent about $20 billion a year and influenced another $200 billion, that is, they influenced the choices their parents make.[15] Thus, they show that the children's market constitutes three markets. James McNeal, who wrote one of the earliest children's marketing textbooks, categorizes the three as current, future (as future buyers), and influential (on their parents' purchases). Getting to children is at the heart of the marketer's fantasy of "cradle-to-grave" marketing in which our entire lifetime is nothing more than a selling opportunity. For McNeal, this ideal is best represented by McDonald's, whose primary targets are, as we all know, children.[16]

The race for the children's market is bitter, as each corporation vies to teach the ever-elusive customer "brand loyalty" as early as kindergarten. It is increasingly common to find advertisements for adult products in children's magazines. On the inside cover of the May 1997 issue of *Sports Illustrated for Kids*, for example, there was a two-page ad for the Chevy Venture minivan. Moreover, children are sold kid-sized models of upscale consumer goods for adults, like cars and clothes. Barbie, that epitome of the suburban consumer, drives a

Porsche, while boys can own models of cars like the Chevrolet and so on. Children are also initiated into the culture of shopping by stores like Libby Lube, a cosmetics store for little girls where they can play at making themselves over.

The market has aggressively entered the school, the second institution after the family that was ideologically constructed to protect children from the market. Some examples: Microsoft tries to get future customers by advertising in schools; Fidelty Investments has put together a package for grade-school children that teaches them money management; Pizza Hut links its promotions to children's performance in school—one free personal pan pizza for meeting the monthly reading quota; Betty Crocker's Traditional Brownie Mix invites children to earn cash for their schools by collecting box tops from all Betty Crocker products; General Mills promises to contribute ten cents for every box top of its cereal; Campbell soup responds by offering money to schools in return for can labels.

Channel One, a ten-minute advertisement program introduced in schools in 1990, best exemplifies the entry of the market into the classroom. The ten-minute programming consists of two minutes of commercials and eight minutes of news. Schools had to agree to ensure that 90 percent of their students would watch Channel One for 92 percent of its airtime. Each program had to be watched in its entirety; teachers could not interrupt the program or turn it off. In return, the schools would get $50,000 worth of equipment, such as television sets, VCRs, and satellite dishes capable of picking up only Channel One. Advertisers considered this captive market so lucrative that they paid more than twice what it cost to advertise on prime-time television. There is a definite class dimension to the dependence of schools on corporate funds: Schools in lower-income neighborhoods are far more dependent than are their upper-income counterparts.

The Post-War Boom: Enter Television

The targeting of children as consumers dates back to the prosperity of the postwar years. During this period, there was a mass-scale improvement in the domestic standard of living, and modern technologies became available to middle- and even working-class homes. Increased middle-class affluence, Barbara Ehrenreich and Henry Jenkins have suggested, coincided with changes in parenting, which became more child centered.[17] Later characterized as "permissive parenting," this approach, Llyod DeMause explains in *The History of*

Childhood, was based on a notion of "helping" children express and live by their own needs. Empathetic parents did not have automatic access to their children's desires but worked hard at trying to understand them. Dr. Benjamin Spock, the chief spokesperson for this position, advised mothers to enjoy their children, not keep rigid schedules, delay toilet training, feed kids on demand, and treat their babies' impulses as valid and legitimate.

It is against this backdrop that television came to play the role of Pied Piper. It was the medium inside the home that advertised toys directly to children over their parents' heads, invested children's products with brand names, encouraged buying more than one of the same toy, and linked children's toys to themes and narratives generated by popular media. Before the advent of television, toy companies spent relatively little on advertising. According to Cy Schneider, they advertised to wholesale toy dealers or to customers through catalogs. National brand names were unknown. About 80 percent of annual toy sales were made in the last three weeks of the year, around Christmas. Large department stores would then set up toy demonstrations to show ways of playing with various toys.

If adults wanted to buy toys, they went to the local toy store and asked for a toy appropriate for a child of a certain age. It is amusing to think what would happen if one tried that in Toys R Us today. We would be faced with shelves of bewildering possibilities, all infinitely similar. This is now a common image even in children's films. Buzz in *Toy Story* finds out that he is a copy by seeing himself advertised on television. In *Monsters Inc.* (2001), remarkably homogenous doors lead into playrooms spread across the continents. In *Artificial Intelligence* (2001), the robotic child finds several copies of itself. In *Toy Story 2* (1999), Buzz finds a whole aisle filled with his likenesses.

It was the Mickey Mouse Club, started by Walt Disney on ABC in 1955, that brought children's commercial television into its own. As Schneider recounts in *Children's Television*, the show initiated the development of a brand (with a recognizable logo), the year-round selling of toys, and the creation of fantastic stories around the toys. Hence toys began to be sold to children in kids' lingo, that is, for the brands and television narratives they were associated with rather than for the functions they could perform. A product's television budget and schedule became almost as important as the toy's charm, particularly in selling to wholesalers, who dominated the toy market in the 1960s.[18] Mattel invented a logo and slogan—"You can tell it's Mattel. It's Swell." As a testimony to the difficulties of convincing children, I would like to offer my friend Chuck Kleinhans's anecdote: He remembers chiming, "You can tell it's Mattel. It smells!"

Investing a product with personality is a way to create brand loyalty, to differentiate one similar product from another, and to weave a web of products, each reinforcing the other. After all, what would differentiate McDonald's from Burger King? Not the food, but the promotional toys associated with films. How else to make one kind of chocolate seem different from another but by humanizing it into a bunch of dancing vaudeville players? Hershey Rollos, according to Schneider, were the first chocolates to have personality. To have been a child in America around the release of the Disney film *Pocahontas* (1996) meant that one would have consumed the film one way or another even without ever seeing it. Before the film's release, department and toy stores were carrying Pocahontas nighties, schoolbags, lunch boxes, sipping cups, pillows, books, and audio tapes. The circular way in which Disney's production of commodities and of culture reinforce each other is a striking example of capitalist expansion. Disney's films provide free advertising for its licensed goods, as well as for its entertainment parks. These commodities in turn provide free publicity for its films. As Richard Schickel noted way back in 1968: "As capitalism it is the work of a genius; as culture it is mostly a horror."[19] Jean Baudrillard, describing these consumption webs as "every marketer's dream," added that "few objects are offered alone, without a context of objects to speak for them. The object is no longer referred to in relation to a specific utility, but as a collection of objects in their total meaning."[20] The goal is to weave such a web of commodities that we depend upon it to define who we are, to indicate and form our identities, and even to protest against it. For instance, the indignation with the meat industry's exploitative practices has spawned an entire food industry targeted to the affluent, health-conscious consumer.

While Baudrillard suggests that this goal has already been realized, it is a contest not yet settled. The industry recognizes that consumers remains elusive, which is why it devotes massive resources to understanding and predicting our behavior.

The cross-referencing between media and toys initiated by Disney is now a fundamental aspect of toy marketing. Approximately 50 percent of the toys produced in 1997, David Leonhardt and Kathleen Kerwin tell us, were licensed toys related to television and film.[21] Children's films are now full-scale pretexts for toys and other children's products. *Toy Story*, for example, came with licensed computer games, breakfast cereal, and McDonald's meals besides each of its characters sold as toys. Barbie, for instance, was never positioned as a doll but invested with the personality of a suburban teenage fashion model. Each early sixty-second Barbie commercial in 1958 told a story about Barbie's life with the invitation to buy new clothes and sets (dream house, beauty salon, etc.) for each new fantasy.[22] The doll's clothing was often more expensive than the doll itself. In 1969 Mattel produced *Hot Wheels*, a TV cartoon series, to advertise a new line of minicars. Government pressure stopped Mattel from advertising the cars on the program, and the show disappeared.

A brief history of television's role in commercializing children's culture shows that, apart from a brief period in the early seventies when television broadcasters self-regulated their presentations under pressure from consumer activist groups such as ACT (Action for Children's Television), television broadcasters have had few restraints.[23] A consistent criticism leveled against television in the sixties was that it was converting children into passive consumers through its repetitive, violent cartoon shows, best exemplified in Federal Communications Commission (FCC) head Newton Minow's 1961 speech that children's programs were "dull, grey, and insipid as dishwater, just as tasteless, just as nourishing."[24]

In 1970 ACT petitioned the FCC to ban toy and food commercials on children's television. In light of these pressures, the National Association of Broadcasters established some rules. First, the host of a television show for children could not appear in commercials; second, commercials on network children's shows would be cut to twelve minutes per hour. But in 1983 under the Reagan administration, FCC chair Mark Fowler deregulated children's television, arguing that it was a business like any other.[25] Since then, children's television has been completely given over to the marketplace.

This boondoggle led to the syndicated show, the program-length commercial, which, as Gary Cross points out, reversed the traditional relationship between a licensed character and a toy. Previously, an entertainment figure like Shirley Temple would spin off toys like Shirley Temple dolls. In contrast, the syndicated program produces first the toy and then the entertainment figure. The best-known shows were *Care Bears* and *Strawberry Shortcake* (Kenner) and *He-man* and *Masters of the Universe* (Mattel). The question of whether children can differentiate between commercials and entertainment programs, so hotly debated in the sixties, has become redundant, as children's films and television are now straightforward pretexts for other market-produced commodities.

Children, the audience of these television commercials-cum-programs, now teach their parents about products available in the market, asking for specific toys. I am reminded of my difficulties as a child in coming up with an answer to the adult question, "What would you like me to get you?" In India in the 1960s, there were the standard things you could buy—candy, dresses, dolls, and some games. Toys were sold in small sections in general stores managed by adults. We just did not know what was on the market. I compare this with my children's experience. The wish lists every year, beginning in preschool, have been packed with the current favorites in the children's market.

The Electronic Pied Piper

It is in directly addressing children as consumers that television acts as the electronic Pied Piper, luring them out of the home and into the street, playing a tune that their parents do not understand. In spite of the gulfs of race, class, and gender, children's consumer culture is central to developing what Ellen Seiter in *Sold Separately* characterizes as the "lingua franca" of small children. It provides formats (such as animation), themes, narratives, and characters around which children communicate with one another. It helps construct the social identity of "child" in opposition to "adult."

Marketers actively work toward building a playful opposition to the adult world into children's consumer culture. Schneider suggests that since children relate to other children, like to feel more grown up, and enjoy ridiculing adult behavior, advertisers should emphasize fun rather than lecture, and stay in the child's cultural world. Even in commercials directed at parents, the joke should be on the contradictory values of the adult and child, with an emphasis on children's enjoyment of the product. For example, in a commercial for Reese's Peanut Butter Cups, the mother goes on about its nutritional value while the kids gobble it up for the taste. Erica Rand in *Barbie's Queer Accessories* recounts that in the preliminary tests for Barbie in the late 1950s, the mothers overwhelmingly hated the dolls, while the girls loved them.

Children's consumer culture has become increasingly unfamiliar to adults. In spite of being a parent of two young children and having a professional interest in children's culture, I find it impossible to keep up and am constantly introduced to new programming and products by my children. In my case, the knowledge gap between me and my children is further widened by the very different economic and cultural environments we come from; whereas I grew up in India in the 1960s and 1970s in a middle-class family, my children were born in the United States. However, the rapid turnover in children's programming on American television leaves most parents in the United States ignorant of what their children are watching.

The gap between the narratives, games, skills, and technologies that we knew as children and those our children know now is vast and continues to grow rapidly. The knowledge gap between adults and children is not closed, as Postman suggests, because of television's disclosure of adult secrets, but widened because of the rapid disappearance of the world adults knew as children. On seeing a typewriter for the first time, my daughter described it as a broken computer. New technologies such as computers that are part of the child's world but new to adults place the child ahead of the adult in achieving a working knowledge of the world. I am also reminded of one of my friends recently telling me about the problems she was having in organizing a family reunion. The older people wanted to get together in a small town in Wisconsin where the father had grown up. The younger people found the town inconvenient, as it did not have an airport and would involve some hours of driving with young children. My friend's point was that the reunion should be organized in a place that was convenient for all. After all, she said, the town existed only in name. None of the old families lived there, and her father's house had long ago been torn down and rebuilt. In her view, her father's attachment to his hometown (not to the reunion) was simply sentimental.

The displacement of older people from the world they knew comes with a lessening of their authority as well. The loss of authority is inscribed in the radicalization of modernity itself. Anthony Giddens explains that the continuing questioning of old knowledge and its replacement with new knowledge is a basic feature of the reflexivity inherent in modernity. He argues that the replacement of religious dogma with rationality necessarily implies that no knowledge is ultimately secure but can be regarded as valid "in principle" only "until further notice."[26]

Once There Was a Family

Not surprisingly, this collapse in adult authority has evoked a conservative clamor for saving the family. As in the mid–nineteenth century, the family is called upon to act as a buffer between the individual and society, to extend childhood, to resist the alienated relations of capitalism, and to be the ground of lasting and loving relationships when all social values are reduced to that of exchange. In this view, television is so threatening because it reaches children in the privacy of the family, inviting them to enter the market as consumers. Parents are asked to resist television through a reassertion of parental authority.

Since the 1980s, there has been a growing concern expressed in child-care books that U.S. children are spoilt and out of control. This view is particularly hostile to parents, especially mothers, whose own experiences are undervalued by the experts. Among others, Lynn Spigel in *Make Room for TV* has discussed the significant increase in the part played by experts in managing domestic life in the post–World War II United States. I had some of this expert-centered child-care phenomenon thrown back upon me during my research. In discussions, mothers were often defensive about the amount of television they allowed their children to watch. It often happened that when I revealed that I was concerned about children and television, not only as a mother but also as a writer on the subject, I would be quickly turned into an expert and asked questions such as these: How much television should children see? Should they see Saturday television at all? Was *Matlida* all right for kids to see? It is a testimony to the power of experts and the lower status of mothers that anyone—teacher, psychologist, principal—is an expert but the mother, who is supposed to execute the rules laid down by the former. It is also symptomatic of the ideology of patriarchal capitalism. While knowledge of the domestic sphere gets increasingly socialized, the responsibility for carrying it out is privatized, with women still assuming the major share.

In keeping with the view that parents are to blame for their children's loss of innocence, Winn and Kline argue that the child-centered parenting practices of the 1960s went too far in giving in to children's unreasonable demands, and they cite television as a prime example. Winn blames "a misplaced pursuit of democracy, a particularly American failing," for the refusal or inability of parents to restrict their children's television viewing. Kline echoes this sentiment when he questions whether "modern 'child-oriented' practices constitute 'liberation'—or the abdication of child-rearing itself."[27]

Kline and Winn hold the view that parents have willfully or otherwise given up control over socializing their children, leaving them to be socialized by television or corporate advertising instead. In what can be read only as a reaction against the women's movement, Winn blames the movement for what she calls women's "flight" from the home, which she claims is in turn precipitated by the "increased willfulness, demandingness, and disagreeableness of undisciplined children" that makes "a life of staying home seem less appealing than the drabbest, most routine office job so many women choose in exchange."[28] Historians such as Barbara Ehrenreich have emphasized that for the majority of mothers, working outside the home is a matter of economic necessity rather than choice. Winn must be talking about only the affluent family that can afford a full-time parent. For this group, then, Winn's attack is on the professional woman's desire for self-realization that extends beyond the roles of mother and wife.

In the rhetoric of reinstating parental authority, the responsibility for restraining children from consumerism is placed on the family rather than on industry. This authoritarian approach is epitomized in short commands: "Shut the set off"; "Take command"; or "No television ever." Acknowledging that authoritarian parenting is a reversal that children, most of all, would resist, Winn concedes that it will be a difficult battle. Yet, she argues, it must be done for the sake of the old family routines—having long dinner conversations, reading books, playing family games, finding common things to do—something she calls "like old fashioned living."[29] She assures parents that once they take the first firm step, their children will follow. She echoes Roald Dahl's 1964 *Charlie and the Chocolate Factory*, published eleven years before her own book, *Plug-in Drug*. Dahl advised parents to throw away the television set and install bookshelves instead. Knowing that the transition would not be easy, he assured parents that once they put up with "all the dirty looks" and

> The screams and yells, the bites and kicks,
> And children hitting you with sticks—
> Then, in about a week or so
> Of having nothing else to do,
> They'll now begin to feel the need
> Of having something good to read.[30]

Dahl conjures up an image, not of a public library but of an upperclass private home furnished with books. The "old-fashioned" family is private, middle class, and strongly marked by hierarchy. Increasingly, instead of suggesting media literacy for children in both the school and the home, as Buckingham and Seiter would recommend, parents are advised that the most important button on the set is the one labeled "off."

Winn and others propose that the family resist capitalism by transforming itself into a private fortress. This is ironic when capitalist expansion (the construction of children as consumers) and new technologies (television and the Internet) drastically challenge the public/private divide on which the family is based. There are two major problems with this view. First, it assumes that consumerism is something imposed on the family. Steven Kline, for instance, argues in *Out of the Garden* that parents are giving up control over children's imaginations to corporations. Similarly, Gary Cross contends that "the conflict between the logic of the market and the rationale of the nurturing family is long and persistent."[31]

While it is true that the family has been *ideologically* constructed in opposition to the market, socialist-feminist historians such as Barrett and McIntosh have consistently pointed out that the family was never outside the relations of the market. The status of the woman and children in the family is contingent upon the bargaining power of the man in the market. Housework and child care were not an escape from the market but supported it and were calculated in the "family wage" paid the male earner. In the absence of the family and the family wage, the worker would not be able to reproduce his labor power. Not only did the family wage buy the male earner freedom from housework (once at home, the man did not work), but the very nature of housework—how one engaged in it—depended upon the man's status in the market.

Walter Benjamin describes the humiliation of economic dependence on husbands and fathers as women and children stood face-to-face with the glittering world of early twentieth-century commodity culture in Berlin:

> In those early years I got to know the "town" only as the theater of purchases, on which occasions it first became apparent how my father's money could cut a path for us between the shop counters and assistants and mirrors, and the appraising eyes of our mother, whose muff lay on the counter. In the ignominy of a "new suit" we stood there, our hands peeping from the sleeves like dirty price tags, and it was only in the confectioner's that our spirits rose with the feeling of having

escaped the false worship that humiliated our mother before idols bearing the names of Mannheimer, Herzog and Isreal, Gerson, Adam, Esders and Madler, Emma Bette, Bud and Lachman. An impenetrable chain of mountains, no caverns of commodities—that was the "town."[32]

The second major problem with the idea that the family can transform itself into a private fortress and thus resist capitalism concerns the fallacy of imagining that corporations impose consumerism on the family. Rather, the primary economic function of the nuclear industrial family was consumption, once production was displaced from the household to the factory. Given that children were constructed as the core of the family, it is hardly surprising that their primary economic role is consumption. When children whine and beg for things in a mall, they are acting out the social and economic role prescribed to them—emotionally valuable but economically dependent amidst a plethora of commodities they cannot buy.

The Discontent of Consumerism

In my discussions with mothers, I found that the drive to "protect" children from consumer culture comes not out of a desire to retain authoritarian control but out of our own discontent with consumerism. Practices such as reading labels on boxes for sugar content, checking ratings on films, or rejecting overpriced, repetitive toys come out of wanting to teach the child to be a critical consumer. My daughter, Suhaila, has often told me how desperately she may want something when we are in Toys "R" Us but once we leave the store it seems not to matter at all. She has talked about the disappointment of buying something and finding it hollow in comparison to the commercial that sold it. When I asked my son's kindergarten class if commercials showed exactly what a toy could do, they all agreed they did not. One woman told me that when she and her children go to the mall, she asks them to make believe they are in a museum—they look, touch, and leave without buying. This position sees both the parent and the child as compatriots in the same world rather than as opponents, with the former having to control the latter. Parents also recognize that the desire to buy things for their children is an expression of love: a desire appropriated by capitalism.

It is against the backdrop of late capitalism and the radicalization of modernity that television plays itself out as the Pied Piper who plays a tune whose lure is incomprehensible to adults; a tune that draws the children irresistibly out of the houses and into the streets and then into a world of which the adults have no knowledge, a world that shuts its doors on them simply because they are adults. Television, as David Harvey points out, does not cause postmodernity to happen.[33] Rather, television is an integral part of postmodernity. It is a symptom, not a cause, of the fundamental changes under way as capitalist expansion and new technologies at the end of the twentieth century fundamentally alter the private/public divide on which the institutions of the family and childhood rest.

There could be a way out of the paralysis of the adults in the Pied Piper story: to stand with our children rather than against them. Which is not to say, as children's marketers tell us, that there are no differences between children and adults. Children are vulnerable physically, and even more so in a society marked by inequality. In spite of the aggressive corporate move to construct children as autonomous, sovereign consumers, children are the most likely to be exploited in the market and susceptible to violence in the family. We know from our own fears of abandonment that being a child on one's own may be an exciting fantasy (because of the freedom it allows from the constraints of school and the family), yet it is a terrifying experience, particularly in a world marked by antagonistic relations of class, race, and gender.

To stand against the market by imprisoning our children under authoritarian control will only alienate us from our children; it is a strategy bound to fail unless we can fly out of the world we live in. The starting point must be a lesson in learning to be a critical consumer. Yet this important first step is still within capitalist relations. To go beyond it, to condemn the turning of children into consumers and workers, we have to reclaim the notion of childhood itself. Children can understand and join us in this critique. They can read labels to see where products are made and can be told that third-world children—children like them—produced them. Children understand the humanist notion underlying childhood, that the small and the weak deserve protection. They are rightfully indignant when an older or bigger child bullies them. They also accept the idea that all children's needs are equal, and they have to be socialized into learning the lessons of class.

I recently took my daughter and her friend, both of whom are fans of the American Girl Dolls (an expensive doll designed as a response to upper-class parents' contempt for Barbie), to the American Girl Store in Chicago around Christmastime. The store, designed as a boutique with attendants every few steps, includes an exorbitantly priced café and a theater, all geared toward establishing as "classy" the status of those who can buy its wares. It was full. As they came out of the store along with others carrying the distinctive red shopping bags, the two girls began talking about how it must feel not to have the money to buy one of those dolls. Don't those of us who received gifts remember the empathy toward the child who could not have them, an empathy that disappears as bourgeois children are socialized to take the inequities of class for granted? Children are quick to see injustice; rather than teach them that capitalist truism, "Life is not fair," we can question life's unfairness.

2 Lost Kingdoms

Little Girls, Empire, and the Uses of Nostalgia

"I think you might do something better with time,"
she said, "than wasting it in asking riddles that
have no answers."
"If you know Time as well as I do," said the
Hatter, "you would not talk about it. It is him."
—Lewis Carroll, *Through the Looking Glass*

When Alice stumbles into Wonderland, she finds herself in a self-enclosed world that appears wildly illogical from a child's point of view. Its inhabitants are obsessed with time, which they see as an autonomous, overwhelming presence that they have to struggle with. Some, like the Hatter, have simply given up the effort. The Hatter's clocks never turn from six and he is always having tea. In contrast to his surrender to time is the queen's frenzied tyranny, bent to the effort of ensuring that things stay on time. She punishes the Hatter for "murdering time" with his rendition of "Twinkle Twinkle Little Bat," commanding, "Off with his head!" As for herself, she tells Alice that in her world, one has to run hard simply to stay in the same place and twice as hard to get somewhere else. In a remarkably visual depiction of the constant novelty yet repetitiveness of modernity and the pressures of time that make childhood and adulthood seem to inhabit two different nations, as it were, Lewis Carroll describes Alice's dizzy feelings as she keeps time with the queen:

> However fast they went, they never seemed to pass anything. . . . And they went so fast that at last they seemed to skim through the air, hardly touching the ground with their

feet, till suddenly, just as Alice was getting quite exhausted, they stopped, and she found herself sitting on the ground breathless and giddy.

Alice looked around her in great surprise. "Why, I do believe we've been under this tree the whole time! Everything's just as it was!"

"Of course it is," said the Queen: "What would you have it?"

"Well, in our country," said Alice, still panting a little, "you'd generally get to somewhere else—if you ran very fast for a long time, as we have been doing."

"A slow sort of country," said the Queen. "Now here, you see, it takes all the running you can do, to keep in the same place. If you want to get somewhere else, you must run at least twice as fast as that!"[1]

It is one of history's dialectics that childhood, itself an invention of modernity, was also imagined as its antidote, as an unchanging state that existed outside time, as if in another country entirely.

Thus imagined as standing outside time and history, childhood became the object of adult nostalgia, not only for a time past but also for a place lost, that is, the home. According to Anne Friedberg in *Window Shopping*, nostalgia is a specific reaction to the temporal and spatial mobility of modernity. Nostalgia, she suggests, in the seventeenth century was a technical term for homesickness: It described longing for a space. By the late nineteenth century, however, it also came to stand for a time past, Friedberg adds, as if to compensate for the shock of the new. Childhood is doubly inscribed with nostalgia, standing for both a lost time and a lost place—a time in one's life and the home where it was spent. In conceiving *Alice in Wonderland* as a gift to a little girl, Lewis Carroll expressed this yearning for a moment in time that was by its nature fragile and fleeting. Alice would certainly grow up into a woman, leaving behind her childhood just as one would a "far-off land."

> Alice, a childish story take
> And with a gentle hand
> Lay it where childhood's dreams are twined
> In memory's mystic band,
> Like pilgrim's withered wreath of flowers plucked in a far-off
>   land.[2]

What has happened to this nostalgia at the end of the twentieth century? Perhaps among the best places to find an answer is in the recent remakes of children's literary classics of the nineteenth century. After all, if childhood is an essential, unchanging experience, children of all ages would enjoy the same cultural artifacts—that is, children's classics, like childhood itself, should never become dated. Such a view, already romantic in the early part of the twentieth century, has now become a marketing strategy. Disney, for example, markets its films from the thirties, such as *Snow White* and *Bambi*, self-proclaiming them "classics." Television advertisements show parents watching these films with their children as a way to share their own childhood with them, as if children's tastes have remained the same over the years. Disney recently extended its commodification of family and childhood to other businesses, like McDonald's; it released through the fast-food chain the toy figurines from Disney's first fifty years. This is a quick drive-through solution to the widespread social critique that fast food is antithetical to traditional family values, one of whose marks was home-cooked meals eaten at leisure. Similarly, old Shirley Temple films re-released in video come with the promise of appealing to today's children just as they had to an earlier generation. These packaged promises of happy childhood memories are directed to adult consumers, relying upon their nostalgia for a time past.

However, remakes or representations of late nineteenth- and early twentieth-century children's literature in the 1990s are just as likely to be characterized by parody as they are by nostalgia. The film *A Simple Wish* (1997), for instance, mocks the idea of a fairy godmother by casting a bumbling, middle-aged man in that role. The same idea is repeated in a recent commercial for toothpaste, with a middle-aged man cast as the tooth fairy. This idea is taken up in the film *Toothless* (1997), where a dentist who was completely devoted to her career and had no desire for family or liking for children finds herself compelled to be a tooth fairy while she waits to be assigned to heaven or hell. The film *Ever After* (1998) locates the Cinderella story in the sixteenth century rather than presenting it as a timeless story and casts the protagonist as a feminist who uses her own wit and courage to rescue herself.

Nostalgia, however, is the dominant response, particularly around narratives that involve young girls and that are marketed to women and girls—for example, the films *Little Women* (1994), *The Secret Garden* (1993), and *A Little Princess* (1995). My questions are: What is the specific nature of nostalgia in these remakes, and what does it tell us about the cultural conception of childhood at the end of the twentieth century? Nostalgia is a concession that something is already past, and it can reveal to us what it is from that past that we seek to redeem in the present.

In this chapter, I look at three versions of *The Little Princess*: first, the original novel by Frances Hodgson Burnett written in 1905; second, its filmed version, *A Little Princess*, starring Shirley Temple and released in 1940; and, finally, the 1995 filmed version of *A Little Princess* directed by Alfonso Cuarón. Burnett (1849–1924) was in her time hugely successful as a writer of novels and plays for adults.[3] However, she is now remembered primarily as a children's writer, as are J. M. Barrie and Lewis Carroll, whose books are key to the Victorian celebration of childhood and its accompanying market in children's fiction. Born in England, Burnett moved to the United States at the age of fifteen. England, however, continued to play an important part in her novels and she traveled often between the two countries. Her first novel, *Little Lord Fauntleroy,* the story of an American child who suddenly inherits an English title and has to win over his stern English grandfather to allow his American mother into the castle, was immensely popular both in England and France. It started, Humphrey Carpenter tells us in *Secret Gardens*, the fashion of dressing up children in velvet dresses with lace collars and doing their hair in ringlets.

Burnett's second popular novel, *The Little Princess*, is the story of Sara Crewe, a young girl who lives in colonial India with her father, a rich businessman. She is sent to an English boarding school for a "proper English" education. Misfortune falls when the father dies of brain fever in India, for all appearances a pauper who had lost his fortune. The hard-hearted schoolmistress, Miss Minchin, strips Sara of all her rich-girl privileges and makes her work as a scullery maid in return for allowing her to continue to live in the school. Finally, Sara's father's friend and business partner, Mr. Carrisford, who has made a fortune with the money invested by her father but is now an old dying bachelor in search of Sara, finds her and transforms her into a princess again by showering her with gifts and riches. Both film versions changed the ending of the novel. In them, the father does not die but is seriously injured and temporarily loses his memory. Eventually, he recovers and the father and daughter end up living happily together.

The theme of a girl child who revitalizes an adult man was repeated in Burnett's third novel, *The Secret Garden*. Mary Lenox, a young girl who is orphaned in India during a cholera epidemic, comes to live in Ireland with her only relative, a reclusive, depressive man who is bereft after his wife's death. Mary is able to return him and his sickly son to life and vitality, just as she restores his dead wife's secret garden to its former beauty.

Childhood in Nineteenth-Century Children's Literature

A thread that runs through the "golden age of children's literature" is the desire on the part of the adult narrator to preserve the child protagonists as "forever children," recognizing at the same time with deep regret that inevitably all children grow up.[4] J. M. Barrie's Peter Pan, Lewis Carroll's Alice, and Burnett's Mary Lenox all have keys that unlock gardens inaccessible to adults. Implicit in Wordsworth's claim that the child was "father of the man" was the notion that the child inhabited a higher spiritual plane than did the adult. In its more drastic versions, the desire to preserve the child in the state of childhood was expressed, according to Carpenter, in a celebration of young children's death.[5]

The notion that the child was a foil to civilization was, as Jean and John Comaroff point out in "Africa Observed," grounded in the contradictory emotions aroused by the Enlightenment. On the one hand, post-Enlightenment confidence viewed both children and the colonized as primitive in evolutionary discourses. On the other hand, critics of the Enlightenment idealized and romanticized children/natives and nature as foils to civilization. Real children had to bear the weight of this modernist projection of children as living outside time. Since childhood was seen as an essential attribute of children, it was imagined that adults could recover that lost state when in the company of children. This sentiment is expressed in Lewis Carroll's letter of thanks to the mother of a young girl: "Many thanks for again lending me Enid. She is one of the dearest of children. It is good for one (the man, for one's spiritual life, and in the same sense in which reading the Bible is good) to come into contact with such sweetness and innocence."[6]

In all of Burnett's novels, children's innocence is premised upon their being completely decipherable to adults. To present the child as transparent, the narrator interjects herself directly into the narrative, interpreting for the reader Sara's every facial gesture and thought and didactically passing judgment on them as good, innocent, charitable, or kind. The story, meant to be read by an adult to a child, presents the adult as an interpreter of the child's thoughts and feelings, which are held to be uncomplicated. For instance, in an episode that depicts Sara's generosity to the children who visited her in the attic during her days as a scullery maid, Burnett lauds Sara's ability to imagine herself in different circumstances. In this particular instance, Sara imagines herself a poor chatelaine who, with nothing left in times of famine, lifts up her spirits by telling stories. Burnett writes that "she was a proud, brave little chatelaine, and dispensed generously the one hospitality she could offer—the dreams she dreamed—the visions she saw—the imaginings that were her joy and comfort."[7] The adult voice continues to this day in literature for very young children (particularly in books aimed at directly socializing the child on issues such as toilet training, going to preschool, and so on). However, children's literature since World War II has tended to erase the voice of the adult narrator and let the characters speak for themselves.

The defining feature of childhood in Burnett's novel is the spiritual grandeur of Sara, who patiently suffers through her impoverishment. This is partly a continuation of the Cinderella motif, where a fallen princess is restored to her earlier status through the intervention of a male savior, the father's friend in this case, who can recognize her innate nobility through the apparent poverty. To this is added the biblical strain in Victorian literature, according to which both women and children must unquestioningly suffer the trials of life so as to be close to God. Sara survives her hardships as a maid by treating her trials as a biblical test of her goodness. As she tells Ermengarde, a somewhat slow child she had befriended earlier: "Perhaps that is what they [the trials] are sent for," to prove if she is a "nice child." In contrast to the money-grubbing schoolmistress, Miss Minchin, Sara has the moral superiority characteristic of a lady. She acts with charity and does not forget her manners even in the poorest of living conditions. On the first page of *The Little Princess*, Burnett writes about the seriousness of Sara, of her "old look" as compared with her young age, for Sara felt "as if she had lived a long, long time."

The paradox at the heart of the bourgeois cult of the beautiful child was that while childhood itself was a privilege of class, the child was supposed to be innocent of class, assuming a spiritual, otherworldly attitude toward money and commerce. Invariably, the child protagonists of these classical narratives were bourgeois. The luxury of childhood, of time spent in play and learning safe within the home and school, away from the factory and the market, was, of course, practically available only to the bourgeois child. The achievement of Charles Dickens was that he highlighted the cruel living conditions and impoverishment of the industrial proletariat through the plight of its children. The fear of slipping down the class hierarchy and finding oneself part of the hordes of working-class children, although trivialized or resolved in bourgeois literature, continued to haunt these mainstream celebrations of childhood as an Edenic state.

From the point of view of children, class privilege was accidental and precarious, dependent as it was so completely on the class status of the father. The dependency of children on adults was certainly not an invention of industrial capitalism. The vulnerability of childhood is expressed in the recurrent motifs of parental abandonment in fairy tales as well. In fairy tales, little children had to be forever on guard, relying on their own cunning to save themselves. What was new to industrial capitalism was the illusion of childhood as a blissful, happy state in spite of the vulnerability of children inside the nuclear family and outside in a public sphere marked by class, gender, and race antagonisms.

Reading these classic childhood texts for their repression of class anxieties reveals the fragility of the construct that childhood was an Edenic state free from economics. Take, for example, Alice as she falls through the rabbit hole into Wonderland. As she is falling, she begins to change size and starts to wonder if she has transformed into someone else. Thinking of all the children her age she knows, she cries in alarm: "I must be Mabel after all, and I shall have to go and live in that poky little house and have next to no toys to play with and oh! ever so many lessons to learn!"[8] Similarly, Sara Crewe, born to a rich businessman but reduced to sharing the attic with Becky, the scullery maid, continues to study late into the night to avert the danger of forgetting her ladylike language. As she says to herself: "I am almost a scullery maid, and if I am a scullery maid who knows nothing, I shall be poor Becky. I wonder if I could quite forget and begin to drop my h's and not remember that Henry the Eighth had six wives" (105). Quite poignantly, she also thinks that it is a mere accident that she was she and Becky was Becky. "We are just the same," Sara tells Becky, "I am only a little girl like you" (56).

One finds in *The Little Princess*, as in other narratives of this genre, detailed descriptions of the lives of wealthy children, thus promoting the emerging market in children's consumer culture. Burnett's second novel, like her first, spends considerable space on the description of her heroine's clothes, thus setting fashion trends in children's clothing, toys, and furniture. The author gives elaborate details, like those found in adult women's novels from the same period, of dresses rich with lace and embroidery, of velvets, gloves, silk stockings, and hats with feathers, including descriptions of clothes for dolls.

Burnett's celebrations of childhood are unabashedly intertwined with the celebration of wealth and privilege. Two of her novels are set in colonial India, where the white children, the narrator gloats, are treated like royalty. Sara lives in a beautiful house surrounded by servants, pets, toys, and "an ayah who worshipped her" (3). She remembers those grand times when she sees Ram Dass (Burnett's spelling), the Indian servant of Lord Carrisford, who moves next door and will eventually rescue her from Minchin's clutches. Burnett writes: "It seemed a strange thing to remember that she—the drudge whom the cook had said insulting things to an hour ago—had only a few years ago been surrounded by people who all treated her as Ram Dass had treated her; who salaamed when she went by, whose foreheads almost touched the ground when she spoke to them, who were her servants and her slaves. It was like a sort of dream. It was all over and it would never come back" (154).

Burnett sets off Sara's superiority by showing her to be unaware of her riches, in contrast to the schoolmistress, Miss Minchin, who is shown to be a greedy spinster. Miss Minchin violates the Victorian code of the spiritual woman encased within the home as wife and mother. She is a single woman who supports herself economically through her school. In contrast to Sara, born into the upper class, Miss Minchin aspires to break away from a lower-middle-class background by copying the mannerisms of privilege, such as speaking French. Her terrible French accent contrasts ridiculously with Sara's, whose mother was French. Miss Minchin is envious of Sara's riches, forbidding Sara to wear lace underwear. However, clearly aware of the prestige money can bring, Miss Minchin resigns herself to letting Sara lead the girls to church so as to build a good impression of her school. Miss Minchin is, Sara thinks, "tall and dull, and respectable and ugly. She had large, cold, fishy eyes, and a large, cold, fishy smile" (7).

In contrast, when Mr. Carrisford moves next door and Sara sees elaborately carved tables of teakwood and even a screen with oriental embroidery, she thinks: "They are beautiful things. They look as if they ought to belong to a nice person. All the things look rather grand. I suppose it is a rich family" (144). A rather straightforward equation is established here between being "nice" and being wealthy. Appropriately, the image Burnett assigns to Sara is that of Marie Antoinette, stripped of her crown and languishing in prison. The cooks under whom she works in the school, the beggar children she is now forced to encounter in the street, the working-class girl, Becky, with whom she is compelled to share the attic, all are presented as primitive and uncivilized. Sara continues to say "May I," "Please," and "Thank you," even when the cooks resent it as "airs and graces" and box her ears and shove her around. Burnett sets Sara apart from the "London savage" who does not even thank her when Sara gives him her bun, although she too is hungry. That street child, Burnett goes on to say, "was only a poor little wild animal" (181). The "good" people are those who can see through to Sara's wealthy lineage in spite of her apparent poverty and are happy to serve her. They are happy to stay in their place, like Ram Dass, who treats her like a raja's daughter, or the woman owner of the bakery, who suspects that Sara is not a beggar and gives her six buns (179).

The novel ends with all the characters in their proper places. Only one little girl is restored to her crown as the little princess. The other girls are settled according to class. Becky becomes Sara's personal maid. The beggar girl to whom Sara had given her buns is employed by the woman who runs the bakery. In fact, class was not transcended even during the unstable middle of the novel. Even when she shares a room with Sara, Becky treats her with deference, acting as her handmaid, helping her dress, and so on. In the most fantastic moment in the story, when Ram Dass, the Indian servant accompanying Mr. Carrisford, transforms Sara's room into one worthy of a princess overnight, Becky's room remains the same. On the following day, Becky is given and a cup so that she can have tea with Sara, and Sara's old mattress to sleep on.

Hollywood's Children

The major change in the transfer of this story to film in 1939 (with Shirley Temple as the star) was that the heavy didactic, judgmental tone of the novel gave way to a socializing rhetoric couched in entertainment aimed not only at children but also at their entire families. The piety of Sara Crewe gives way to the cuteness of Shirley Temple. Positioning the Shirley Temple films as made "for" families not only made good business sense but also gained respectability for cinema.

The film at first glance appears to do away with the voice of the narrator, the adult voice that interprets the events for the child reading the novel or having it read to him or her. Instead, the cinematic conventions of invisible editing sustain the illusion for both adult and child that they can directly read Sara's thoughts. The casting of the viewer as subject is a fundamental insight of psychoanalytic film theory, particularly the work of Christian Metz.[9] Shirley Temple's acting and the myths that surrounded her performance further reinforced this transparency. In "Shirley Temple and the House of Rockefeller," Charles Eckert's analysis of the publicity that surrounded Shirley Temple shows that the making of her films was consistently represented as all play and no work; the films were made almost by themselves, spontaneously and naturally. This publicity made the ten thousand dollars a week that Shirley earned during the depression seem a miracle rather than a fact of commerce.

In investigating why Shirley Temple's films were treated with such indulgence and affection, as if they were children themselves, and are now marketed in the same way, it is important to see how they depend upon earlier notions of children as innocent and knowable. This direct access to children is built into the films not only in their themes but also in the ways in which children were constructed as objects of—building upon Laura Mulvey's discussion of the male gaze—what we can describe as the adult gaze. Mulvey argued in "Visual Pleasure and Narrative Cinema" that mainstream cinema compelled the viewer—man or woman—to view women as objects of male sexual consumption by adopting what she characterized as the "male gaze." Viewers were brought into the film by identification with the gaze both of the camera and of the male actors in the film, which viewed women as objects of heterosexual male scopophilic desire.

The adult gaze presents the child as an innocent object, transparent and uncomplicated, blissfully unaware of being watched by an adult audience. The conventions of performance for the child actor demanded this transparency. Child stars were supposed to be not acting but being themselves, and Shirley Temple, the biggest child star of all, had perfected the ability to make manifest all the inner thoughts and emotions of a character (which supposedly was no other than Shirley Temple in various situations, because as the quintessential child she remained the same). Her face was an open book that brought to the surface her uncomplicated emotions. For instance, the close-up on her face as she is told about her father's death in *A Little Princess* tells us exactly what she is thinking—first denial, then shocked acceptance, then the conviction that he is not dead, and finally the resolve to find him.

The camera also offers Temple's innocence to the audience by making us privy to her thoughts and actions when she imagines herself to be alone. For instance, voyeuristically we watch her talk to the horses or to her shoe, maintaining the pretense that the child is really being herself and not performing for us; such scenes are similar to gratuitous scenes of women taking showers, supposedly unaware of being watched. The adult gaze is also maintained through identification with the adult characters in the film who look at the child actor—the camera lingering on their adoring faces as they watch Shirley Temple after she is out of the frame—and exchange glances that emphasize her cuteness. A predominant part of Temple's performance is entertainment, through her dances, songs, and jokes. Yet Temple is entertaining not just when she is singing or dancing and therefore obviously performing for an adoring adult audience, but even more when she is supposedly alone, being herself.

The image of the child star was an important institution in upholding the idea of children's innocence, which in turn came in handy when building national resolve during the depression years. The twenties and thirties were the decades of the child star—Baby Peggy, or Diana Cary, in the early twenties; Jackie Coogan, who was made famous playing opposite Charlie Chaplin in *The Kid* (1920); Shirley Temple, whose name could carry a film all on its own; Mickey Rooney, Jane Withers, Dickie Moore, and Stymie of the *Our Gang* series; Roddie McDowell; and Fredie Bartholomew. The child-star era played itself out between the two wars, never to revive. The nineties saw a return of children as actors and performers, not as stars, as children's roles have become more nuanced and children's separation from adults broken down.

What is of significance for our discussion is that in the interwar years, Hollywood mass-produced and sold the nineteenth-century idealization of the child. The star, Richard Dyer suggests in "Heavenly Bodies," highlights the contradictions between self and society produced in capitalist society. The star image, created by Hollywood through publicity and other industries that thrive off the entertainment business, is so fascinating to us, Dyer argues, because it holds up the belief that there is an authentic self to be found underneath the public persona, a belief that reassures us that we in turn are living an authentic life. For instance, gossip magazines make a great deal of their effort to show us stars doing everyday things like shopping or changing diapers; we continue to be riveted by these details because our belief in the existence of an authentic self for the star and ourselves is precarious, even as it is so intensely desired.

The image of the child star, however, drawing upon the ideological construction of childhood as the last authentic state left in capitalism, could be consumed without guilt. The culture industry held on to this image ferociously, placing child stars above criticism, as if to criticize a child's performance was to criticize childhood itself. Twentieth Century Fox filed a libel suit against Graham Greene, who, commenting on the flirtatious and sexualized performance of Temple, had written that she merely wore a mask of childhood that, although clever, was short-lived, for she would grow into a woman. Her admirers, he remarked—"middle aged men and clergy men—respond to her dubious coquetry, to the sight of her well-shaped and desirable little body, packed with enormous energy, only because the safety curtain of story and dialogue drops between their intelligence and desire."[10] Greene's argument that Temple's innocence was a sexual ploy is commonly accepted now; by attributing it to Temple's performance, Greene failed to see that it was already an old phenomenon, a continuation of the Victorian sexualization of young girls. James Kincaid writes in "Producing Erotic Children" that innocence is the cornerstone of the ideological system that produces erotic children. Therefore, Shirley Temple stopped being enticing once she hit puberty.

The notion that Shirley Temple did not play roles in her films but that she was simply being herself—that her films were, as we have noted, produced spontaneously, even when Shirley Temple could hold her own with adult dancers like Bill Robinson—depended on the notion that the public and private selves were seamlessly connected in children. Consequently, child stars were not supposed to be working, only playing. Publicity was spun about the naturalness of these performers and conscious efforts made to not let them "grow up." Charlie Chaplin, idealizing his self-image as the tramp in *The Kid*, said about its star, Jackie Coogan:

> Ah, Jackie, wonderful Jackie! Jackie is inspiring and inspired. Just to be in his presence is to feel inspired. His personality is beautiful, lovely. It's spiritual. You feel close to his spirituality. . . . The essential thing is to keep his mind clear of all

opinions, prejudices, creeds, religions and manufactured thoughts. It is such a fine sensitive mind, it mustn't be twisted. I don't like seeing him attending Chamber of Commerce banquets, press luncheons and such, sitting at the head of the table receiving homage and applause.[11]

Shirley Temple later recounted to fellow former child star Dick Moore that she always had lunch by herself in her bungalow: "I wasn't supposed to mix with adults. I was supposed to be kept a child. They figured that if I had lunch in the commissary I would learn jokes and I would become a little adult, which they didn't want."[12]

Biographies and some autobiographies of child stars began to appear in the late seventies aimed precisely at shattering the myth of the child star as a playful innocent.[13] Former child stars talked about their "stolen childhoods"—the pressure to compete with other children; the isolation from other children and adults, as they were to be kept childlike as long as possible; the relentless pressures of work; dieting; lying about their age; providing for the luxuries and extravagance of their parents, who eventually betrayed them. Jackie Coogan as an adult sued his mother and stepfather, leading to the passage of the Coogan law in California in June 1939, which mandated that a court could demand that up to half the income earned by a child be kept in a trust for the child until he or she attained maturity. Child-labor laws were applied to the film industry as well, and child actors were supposed to attend three hours of school between eight and four. Studios, therefore, had a teacher on the premises who taught the children across different grades and subjects, all in one class.[14]

Child Star as Commodity

The child-star phenomenon initiated the mass marketing of children's consumer culture and of childhood as a commodity, a practice that would blossom after World War II. Jackie Coogan had pencil boxes, lunch pails, and chewing gum licensed in his name. He received $50,000 yearly for the use of his photograph on an Erector Set. His name was on a line of expensive children's clothing. There were Jackie Coogan dolls and chocolates. Similarly, there were Shirley Temple dolls, handbags, sewing cards, paper dolls, coloring books, and soaps. Shirley Temple's *Captain January* (1936) was made to coincide with her birthday, and it came with a licensed book, a practice common for children's films now. Department stores ran Shirley look-alike

contests and advertised her movies in their stores, while movie theaters set up Shirley Temple doll displays in their lobbies. There were
Baby Peggy dresses, purses, dolls, prunes, and even spinach. Jane
Withers's name was merchandised on paper dolls, dresses, hair bows,
socks, shoes, and, gloves.[15] After the Second World War, the child star
would be replaced by the animated character. Not only was this more
cost efficient, since studios retained the rights over animated characters, but also the animated character did not age, unlike the child star,
whose market value fell every year.

The child star granted respectability to cinema as it consolidated
itself as a business through the studio system in the twenties and thirties and worked its way upward from being an entertainment form for
the working class and immigrants. It also provided ideological justification, as Eckert has argued in regard to the Shirley Temple image
in "Shirley Temple and the House of Rockefeller," for the inadequate
measures taken by the state to alleviate the poverty of the depression
years. The child in a film, when used to justify thrift and delayed gratification to the poor, could be a deeply conservative ploy during the
depression. Eckert outlines the major theme of the Shirley Temple films
as a motherless child who through her love wins over the rich and
eccentric into giving charity to the poor. Her image attempted to generate hope that the future would be good if only the present could be
borne with humor and faith.

Child stars served as political mascots as well. Baby Peggy was
the mascot of the 1924 Democratic convention, and FDR said: "As long
as our country has Shirley Temple we'll be all right."[16] Typically, these
children held up as noneconomic tropes were the only earning members of their families. Their earnings sustained their families' extravagant Hollywood lifestyles, in contrast to the squalor in the streets during
the depression years. As adults, these former stars began to expose in
their autobiographies the cynicism and hypocrisy underlying the image of the playfully innocent child. Perhaps their indignation was fu-
elled by the knowledge that they were used to sell an image which
they were not allowed to live out.

In this early attempt by Hollywood to mass market childhood, we
can already discern the homogenization and simplification of children's
culture, as childhood got branded sweet and cuddly, cute and tiny.
Teddy bears were transformed from frightening animals into cuddly
ones, and the screen persona of the stars presented the child as directly knowable and uncomplicated beings. The romantic celebration

of the child as spiritual and otherworldly, a mystery to the adult and also the savior of the adult, was giving way to cute and cuddly toy, which could also be owned by an adult. Shirley Temple's cuteness is a diminution of Sara Crewe's spiritual superiority. While Shirley Temple's Sara was supposed to invoke adult indulgence, Frances Burnett's Sara had sought to invoke adult awe and adoration.

Childhood as an Antique

The 1995 film *A Little Princess* presents a strikingly different image of Sara. Its elaborate artifice stages girl children like Sara and stories like *A Little Princess* as antiques, things from a time that is past and lost. While both the novel and the 1939 film present Sara's story in a realist style, the 1995 film shapes itself as a highly crafted fairy tale through elaborate mise-en-scène, composition, and editing. Green predominates in the color composition of the film, as green filters are used throughout. Sets are elaborately mounted to present a world that is dated and also one that is seen from the point of view of a child. The door knobs are higher and bigger; Miss Minchin is made to appear very tall through a low-angle shot when Sara sees her for the first time; Ram Das is dressed like an Indian maharaja or magician whose appearance is accompanied each time by a musical tune; and the intercutting between the lives of the father and daughter is highly symbolic.

The elaborate mise-en-scène and composition evoke the grandeur of fairy tales and, at the same time, a reflection on the institution of childhood itself. Take, for instance, the way the director, Alfonso Cuarón, stages the moment at which Sara learns of her father's death. It is Sara's birthday and Miss Minchin has organized an elaborate party, expecting to be handsomely remunerated by Sara's father. At the exact moment that Sara bends to blow out the candles on her cake, her father's lawyer enters the school to inform Miss Minchin of the catastrophic change in Sara's life. The fall from being a princess is sudden and swift as the child becomes a victim of circumstances beyond her control. The film visually mourns this loss as we see the heartbreaking beauty of Sara blowing out the candles. The lawyer lingers briefly by the door of the room where the party is in process, a passive bystander standing in for the world that would permit a child's life to be subjected to the harsh deprivations of poverty without lifting a finger. The film inserts these detached moments of reflection upon the institution of childhood, viewing it with the eyes of the present

2.1. As Sara blows out the candles, she is also unknowingly blowing away her life as she has lived it so far.

as a thing of the past, thus investing Burnett's story with a self-conscious adult point of view that the original lacked. Consequently, the film also speaks to adults, drawing us into a fragmented identification both with the children and with a detached contemplation of the meaning of childhood itself. (A similar move is apparent in Cuarón's direction of the third in the *Harry Potter* film series. Cuarón invests the film, unlike the first two in the series, with the trials and trauma of growing up.)

The narrative element that transforms this version of *The Little Princess* into a fairy tale is the recasting of the story as the Hindu epic Ramayana. There are several versions of the Ramayana, but an element common to them is the adventures of the Hindu god Rama; his wife, Sita; and his brother, Laxman, during a long period of exile imposed on Rama by his stepmother. During the exile, Sita is kidnapped by a demon, Ravana. Rama and Laxman then wage war against Ravana and rescue Sita. The Ramayana serves as the core around which Sara's imaginative life, her close bond with her father, and the mounting of the film as a fairy tale are set. We are brought into the film in its opening scene as an intimate circle of listeners around a young girl who is a compelling storyteller. With the screen blank and green, we hear a little girl's voice narrate to the sound of a sitar: "A very long time ago there was a beautiful princess in a mystical land called . . . India." On the screen appears an old yellowing map with INDIA written across it. The next shot opens from a small iris to reveal a brightly colored image of a man and woman in the style of Indian miniature paintings. This is the beginning of the story of the Ramayana, which establishes Ram and Sita as lovers who lived in exile alone in the enchanted forest. We will learn later that the man cast as Rama is Sara's father and the Ramayana is the imaginative thread that binds father and daughter together through their struggles while apart.

It's the Father's Story

Adult nostalgia is foregrounded in the 1995 version of *A Little Princess* by the central significance of the father to the narrative, so much so that the father emerges as the protagonist of the story, which had started out as a tale about the trials of a young girl. Bruno Bettelheim in *The Uses of Enchantment* has argued that in the classical fairy tale motif, the child protagonist is dislocated from a home to which she or he returns at the end a different person, no longer dependent on the parents. This pattern fits the journey Captain Crewe, Sara's father, makes in the 1995 version of the story. The fathers in the novel and the 1939 film are mere bystanders—their absence provides causality to the story, while the story centers on Sara's trials. In the novel, Crewe is a "rash, innocent young man who wanted his little girl to have everything that she admired and everything that he admired himself" (10). He dies quite early in the novel and is replaced by his friend and business partner, Carrisford, who continues the search for Sara until he finds her. In the 1939 version as well, Crewe is absent through all Sara's trials as a scullery maid. We have no account of what happens to him at war. The story ends once Sara finds him, delirious and amnesiac, in a military hospital. There is no interest in the narrative in exploring how the father had experienced his loss of memory.

In contrast, the father in the 1995 version is the grandest of all. His dislocation from India/home and his loss of memory are as central to the narrative as are Sara's dislocation from India/home and abandonment by her father. In retelling the Ramayana, Sara casts her father as Rama and herself as Sita. In an interpretation of the Ramayana as a Western-style romantic fairy tale, Crewe, always upright and dressed formally in military uniform, is Prince Charming.

2.2. On her last night with her father in India, Sara's room is cast in a golden hue.

In Cuarón's film, Sara and her father's troubles begin when they have to leave India, as Crewe is called to fight in the First World War. On their last night in India, Crewe, like King Ram, looks out his window, surveying his kingdom for one last time. He tells his daughter that she will always be his little princess, words that will sustain Sara through the trials that are to follow. The mise-en-scène highlights the palatial character of Sara's bedroom, which is luxurious and predominantly golden, setting up the misery of exile in its contrast with the dull greens that dominate the latter part of the film. India has so far been shown as a beautiful, placid land of waterfalls, sunsets and rivers, fog and mist.

Crewe's exile from India is presented as a personal quest, quite like a hero's banishment from home and not a quest for national glory. Unlike the 1939 film, there is no glorification of war or celebration of British victories. Instead, war is shown as intrinsically destructive. Crewe is injured in the war and loses his memory. This loss is alarming for Sara; it is an abysmal loss for Crewe. In fact, Crewe gives a deeply felt account of nostalgia. His memory is stirred when he first hears a Hindi word. Crewe describes the feeling it arouses as "a strange sensation—feeling your heart remember something that your mind cannot." From Crewe's point of view, the narrative is the regaining of his lost kingdom. The two things he loses, those that make him stand kingly and proud, are India and Sara.

The Lost Kingdom: India

The father longs for India not as a source of wealth or status but as an inspiration to the imagination. The transition to nostalgia progresses historically through the three versions of *The Little Princess*. The novel was written three decades after India was formally made part of the British Empire, which took over control from the East India Company in 1857. India in the novel is a source of fabulous wealth. The fact that Sara's father has diamond mines there establishes her status as princess in the boarding school. But in itself, India is presented as an inhospitable place not fit for children.

Burnett's novels provided ideological justification for apartheid, the foundation of colonialism. Apartheid served both an ideological and an economic function. Ideologically, it propped up the colonizers as the "master race," justifying the exclusion of Indians from political and economic power. It could be sustained only through marked racial segregation, made possible by the setting up of British homes in India. It fell upon British women and children to create these homes as an exclusive private sphere markedly different from the native culture—hence the emphasis on manners and dress, ways of speaking, ritual and custom in these colonial texts. Before 1857, men of the East India Company were apt to marry native women and adopt indigenous modes of dress and food, often mimicking the local kings or landlords.

British homes in India not only helped maintain imperial rule but also provided a justification for its existence: British women and children had to be protected from the natives. In Burnett's novel, Sara's departure from India is precipitated by her mother's death. Burnett writes that India was unsuitable for British children, who were either made sick by the weather or turned into imbeciles by the constant pampering of the Indian servants. British children could get a "correct" education only in England. For Sara, leaving India is not a catastrophe imposed by external circumstances but an inevitable part of growing up British in India.

In the 1939 film version, India is marginal to the story. By this time, the Indian national movement had already supported two major movements of civil disobedience. Gandhi had agreed to support

the British in the war on condition that India would be given sover-
eignty after the war. The British were holding on, but the empire was
clearly under threat. This seems to explain the absence of India as a
source of wealth in this version. India is mentioned only once in the
film. On her birthday, Sara is given a picture of India by Miss Minchin.
Sara thanks Miss Minchin, saying that now she will not have to try
"so hard" to remember India. India is still a possession, a colony, not
yet an object of nostalgia. Instead, Sara's imaginative life is full of Western imagery of elves and fairies. In one sequence, Sara dressed as an
angel gets her teacher married by granting her wish to kiss her suitor.
Further, the narrative is preoccupied with generating patriotic support
for nation building in the United States, making India a remote consideration. Sara imagines herself to be a little soldier (an element that
is in the original novel but highly exaggerated here). From tying her
shoes to coping with the news of her father's death, Sara deals with it
all like a soldier's daughter.

In the 1995 version, however, India is transformed from a material place of wealth to a source for the imagination, a projection of
the father and daughter's longing for the past. Ramayana/India becomes
the device that sets up the powerful, almost otherworldly, character
of Sara's imagination and her ties to the father. Sara begins her story
with Ram and Sita, who, although in exile, live happily in the enchanted forest, just like she does with her father in India. She pauses
her story at Sita's kidnapping by Ravana as she herself moves to New
York. The next time she returns to the story, Sara is in Miss Minchin's
boarding school. Now she tells about the imprisonment of Sita by the
demon, Ravana, in a green tower on top of a hill. Rama comes to her
rescue but is trapped amidst Ravana's deadly weapons. As Sara nar-
rates this story, it is superimposed over scenes of her father fighting a
desperate battle to survive. Ravana's poisonous weapons correspond
with the fumes of war in which Crewe is trapped.

At this point, Miss Minchin interrupts the narrative to tell Sara
that her father has died in the war. As Sara faces this calamity, we are
shown a striking visual rendering of the closeness of father and daughter as also the power of the imagination. Alone in the attic, Sara finds
a little piece of chalk. With it she draws a circle in which she curls
up in a fetal position, crying out, "Papa" in desolation. The camera
pulls out, showing the gothic green tower of the boarding school, in-
voking the tower in which Ravana holds Sita captive. The circle Sara
draws evokes the Laxman Rekha and the circle drawn by Laxman

2.3 and 2.4. The shot of Sara's father enveloped in the smoke and flames of World War II dissolves into a shot of Rama enveloped by poisonous flames.

around Sita when he left her to look for Rama, telling her that she will be safe as long as she stays inside the circle.[17] Sara's life makes a turn for the better on the night she tells the story of Rama's victory over Ravana. Sara and Becky wake up to a room beyond their wildest imaginings. They are covered in warm blankets, luxurious gowns and slippers wait for them, and the table is laid out with a feast of a breakfast.

Edward Said in *Orientalism* has argued that the Orient is not a geographical location but an ideological construct on which the West projects its anxieties and desires. In the 1995 version of *A Little Princess*, India is the Other, with its differences reduced to a few recognizable stereotypes: Ram Das is dressed like a rajah; a large Buddha head, lattices, and the Taj Mahal signify the landscape; and a ten-headed Chinese dragon stands for Ravana. As a mystic place, it is, as Crewe says, a land "that stirs the imagination, like no other place in the world." Remembering India, even for Sara, a child, is an exercise of the mind. She does not teach the other children at her boarding school any Indian games or talk about the foods and the smells of India. It takes a working-class child, Becky, to make Sara concretize her memories of India. She presents Sara with a pillow on her birthday. On the pillow, Becky has embroidered rivers, mountains, and trees from India, imagining them from Sara's stories. Becky asks Sara to tell her about India. "Does the air taste like coconuts?" she asks. Sara, her hands caressing the embroidery, answers, "No, it's more like spices, really—curry and saffron."

The extent to which India becomes an abstraction or an object of nostalgia by the 1995 version is made clearest by the role played by Ram Das in the three versions. In Burnett's novel, Ram Das is Mr. Carrisford's servant, a subservient "native." When Sara sees him for the first time, she is reminded of her ayah, who worshipped her. Ram Das treats her like a rajah's daughter, carefully averting his "native" eyes when he sees the bare room in which she lives. Although it is Ram Das who physically transforms Sara's attic room into a comfortable, warm place, it is Carrisford who is given credit for it. Ram Das is merely a conduit, using his "native soft-footed agility," Burnett writes, to enact Carrisford's generosity. Burnett, compelled to remark on the supposed anomaly of Ram Das as the god-fairy, writes that "it would have been a fairy tale other than that it was made to come true by an Oriental!" (264). In the 1939 film, Ram Das continues to be servile and introduces himself as the servant of Lord Wikham, who is always curt

and short with him. He too transforms Sara's room on Wikham's orders. In both these versions, Ram Das is an insecure, timid, and obse-
quious man who is only too grateful to Sara for her attention.

Ram Das undergoes a major transformation in the 1995 version.
Instead of the servile native of the earlier versions, he is the personal
guru of Lord Randolph, as well as Sara's fairy godfather. Dressed like
a magician or a rajah, he embodies wisdom and far-sightedness. He
first appears on the screen on the first night Sara is away from India
aboard the ship on her way to America. He stands alone not as an attachment to a white man but as a guardian angel watching over her.
Every time he comes in the frame with Sara, a great wind draws her
to him. On one of her bleakest days, a strong wind blows her shawl away.
She follows the shawl and ends up at Ram Das's feet. The camera looks
up from her point of view at Ram Das's majestic frame and kind eyes.

Sara has a deeply spiritual relationship with Ram Das, one which
is built around the imagination—a relation that most closely resembles
what she shares with her father. The magical, otherworldly, and deeply
joyful nature of the bond between Ram Das and Sara is communicated
through the highly crafted imagery around their meetings. The first
night that Sara begins telling the stories again, to Becky in the attic,
the door to their room opens and the wind and snow rush in. Sara
walks out in the snow and sees Ram Das, who smiles at her and raises
his hands, and she swirls in the snow. His eyes are closed. The sound
track plays "Take My Heart." Ram Das bends down in greeting, and
so does Sara. He raises his hands. So does she. In this narrative, Ram
Das is unequivocally Sara's fairy godfather, magically transforming her
room from a scullery maid's to that of a princess. Even more importantly, it is Ram Das who revives Crewe, almost willing him to remember Sara before she is taken away by the police and is lost to him
forever.

The Lost Kingdom: Little Girls

The second fundamental element in Crewe's recov-
ery is his recognition of Sara. In its representation of the girl child,
the film falls back on the Victorian idealization and eroticization of
prepubescent girls. Jackie Wullschlager has argued in *Inventing Wonderland* that the Victorian suppression of female sexuality found an
outlet in the idealization of the little girl, who was, in turn, epitomized
as a model for pure adult women. The chaste adult Victorian woman,
like the child, was idealized as dependent and as an erotic object who

did not demand sexual satisfaction in return. There is in the three versions a remarkable continuity in presenting the young girl as a romantic object. However, by the 1995 version, this can be presented only nostalgically rather than normatively.

In the novel, Burnett writes unselfconsciously of Sara's pride in being her father's "little missus" or refers to them as "the dearest of friends and lovers in the world." Sara suffers the separation from her father and goes to the boarding school so that she can learn to take care of her father as an ideal Victorian wife would. She longs to "take care of her Papa, . . . to keep the house: to ride with him, and sit at the head of his table when he had dinner parties; to talk to him and read his books" (4). After her father's death, the role of the adoring older man is taken on by his friend Carrisford, who adopts Sara. On discovering Sara, Carrisford, who so far had been a sickly, disenchanted man, is suddenly revitalized. He is completely preoccupied by romancing Sara, who now finds "beautiful new flowers growing in her room, whimsical little gifts tucked under pillows" (274). Adult women are presented as sensible and matronly or greedy and materialistic. It is the young girl who is the object of desire, as a "pure" entity in a harsh, materialistic world. Carrisford cares nothing for the huge fortune he has acquired until he has Sara to spend it on.

In the Shirley Temple film, this idealization of young girls is displaced onto adult women. The ideal adult women are like little girls— virginal objects of admiration and desire. The 1940 film introduces a new subplot, a romance between a teacher, Miss Rose, and Geoffrey, the riding master. Miss Rose is a chaste, virginal, dutiful young woman whose kisses for Geoffrey never slide into passion. On top of this world of little girls and chivalrous men sits Queen Victoria, who is no other than an old little girl. In the climax of the film, Sara runs into the military hospital looking for her father among the wounded. It is already past visiting time and Miss Minchin has sent the police after her. As she struggles to break free from the hold of a sergeant who has caught her, a squeaky, little-girl voice asks, "What is it that the child wants?" The reverse shot is of Queen Victoria surrounded by men in military uniform. As Sara gets the idea that she may be talking to the queen, she asks, "What is your name?" "Victoria," replies the queen, revealing herself as the little girl she really is, and asks, "What's yours?"

The 1995 version is the most explicit in depicting the father-daughter relationship as a romantic one. It is the father who transforms his daughter into a princess, a privilege not granted to all girls. In Sara's profoundest confrontation with Miss Minchin, when the latter asks her to stop believing she is a princess, Sara replies: "I am a princess. All girls are. Even if they live in tiny old attics, . . . even if they dress in rags. . . . Even if they aren't beautiful, or smart, or young, . . . they are still princesses. All of us. Didn't your father ever tell you that? Didn't he?" In a remarkable scene, which translates the change in status visually and not just through dialogue, the camera angle shifts from looking up at Minchin to looking down upon her and ends on a close-up of her devastated face.

More than either of the earlier versions, the 1995 film presents the romantic ideal as the little girl's oedipal fantasy of replacing her mother in her father's life. Sara casts Crewe as Rama and herself as Sita in a fairy tale of Prince Charming rescuing a stranded princess. While it is Sara's mother who plays the role of Sita—one suspects, to insure a PG rating—the logic of plot development, the parallels in the father's and daughter's lives, and the romantic nature of their relationship cast Sara as her father's Sita. First, on their way to New York, Crewe gives Sara the locket he had given her mother on their wedding night. Mounted beautifully as an elaborate romantic fantasy, this scene is set on a huge white ship hit by large white waves, with both the father and daughter dressed very formally in white and dancing what seems a wedding dance.

Adult male desire for young girls is projected onto the little girl by attributing the romantic fantasy to her, casting the daughter as the desiring subject. Since the child is presumed to be innocent, her desire for her father is represented as natural and therefore not sexually demanding the way an adult woman's would be. This displacement resonates with women as well, as Julia Lesage has shown, in a complex reading of women's fragmented consciousness in relation to incest, which, she posits, is born out of the social structures of patriarchy. Women are attracted to the oppressor because they can identify with and understand the abuser's exercise of his lust, and also desire the power granted to men. "So long as," Lesage states directly, "my sexual object choice has more social valorization or income or strength than I do, and this is a systemic aspect of the structure of desire, feminine identification with stories of abuse makes sense."[18] Cuarón crafts his narrative with the oedipal romance as its emotional spine and casts Sara as the narrator, thus replacing Burnett's sentimentality with a complicated contest between masculinist desire for passive women and young women's own imaginative entry into patriarchal culture.

The dominant theme, however, is the idealization of the adoring and sexually undemanding girl child as the model for the adult woman. Subsequently, adult womanhood is seen as a fall from grace. In the 1995 version, Miss Minchin is presented as a worldly, greedy woman who therefore lacks the ability to be loved, while her sister, Amelia, is made an object of ridicule. Miss Minchin stands for the commercialized world in which there is no place for fantasy. She tells Sara to give up her ridiculous fantasies and be productive and useful. The film's only romantic relationship between adults is presented as a comic moment. Amelia is a fat, timid woman. Sara, knowing that Amelia has a crush on Francis, the milkman, urges her to elope with him to some exotic place. The night Amelia elopes, she first throws down one suitcase on top of Francis, then another. Finally, she comes crashing out the window backside out, right on top of him, the exact antithesis of delicate princesses protected by men. It is the little girl and the Indian woman, Maya, who are represented as the feminine ideal. Maya is the first to tell the story of the Ramayana to Sara and speak to her about love. Unlike the Western adult woman, Maya, the noble savage, is close in spirit to that of the child.

The Uses of Nostalgia

Alice could run along with the queen but see her frenzied pace as ridiculous because, in 1865, children were imagined as living outside the grasp of time. In showing Sara Crewe to be a girl from another time, Alfonso Cuarón's 1995 film nostalgically looks back at an era when little girls (and women) looked up to kingly fathers (and men), and parts of the world existed as material for the white man's imagination (a phenomenon that still lingers). Is there anything liberating in this nostalgic construction? Susan Buck-Morss, reading Walter Benjamin, writes that not all nostalgia is reactionary. Some images from the past are called up in the present to redeem utopian desires lost in history. These redeeming images from the past represent the collective desire for an end to scarcity, and in seeking them, humanity acts like the child who learns the practical task of grasping by trying to catch the moon.[19] I would suggest that in the nostalgia of the 1995 version of A Little Princess, there is a desire to redefine the parent-child relationship as one of the heart and the imagination, rather than as one of money.

The 1995 version reclaims the parent-child bond as economically valueless but deeply spiritual and emotional. In a fundamental departure from the earlier versions, Sara's imagination is not intrinsic to Sara but is a gift from her father. In contrast to the fathers in both the novel and the 1939 film, who shower their Saras with all kinds of material gifts—dresses, dolls, and even a pony—the father in the 1995 version gives his daughter the gift of imagination.

In the 1995 version, Crewe gives three gifts to his daughter. The first of these is the Ramayana. He gives her a copy of the book on their last night in India. The Ramayana stands for both their shared personal history in India and the bond that connects them. When Miss Minchin reduces Sara to the life of a maid, she lets her keep "the Book" because she has no clue of its worth to Sara. The second gift that Crewe gives his daughter is the locket that he had given her mother on their wedding night. Of all his gifts, this is the only one that has any commercial value. Subsequently, it is the locket that Miss Minchin grabs from Sara when she hears of Crewe's death.

The third gift he gives Sara is the doll Emily. How Emily comes alive in the three versions is central to understanding the role played by the father in developing Sara's imagination. In both the novel and the 1939 version, it is Sara's imagination that makes the doll come alive. Burnett writes that Sara had imagined a doll called Emily even before she had seen her. In her last days in London, before her father leaves for the war, he takes her on a long shopping trip, buying her all kinds of fancy dresses. In one of the shop windows, Sara spots a doll that she insists is Emily as she has imagined her. Her father indulges her fantasy by saying, "Dear me, I feel as if we ought to have someone to introduce us" (12). The narration further reinforces the idea that Emily's specialness is a product of Sara's imagination. Burnett writes: "Perhaps she [Sara] had known her. She [Emily] had certainly a very intelligent expression in her eyes when Sara took her in her arms" (11). This is the adult watching the child's imagination with wonder. In the 1939 film version, Emily is a doll ordered by Sara's father all the way from France. On seeing her, Sara reassures her father that she will be all right with a friend as understanding as Emily, one who has such an "intelligent-looking forehead." In both these versions, it is Sara who weaves stories around Emily.

By contrast, in the 1995 version, Sara's imaginative life around Emily is a gift from her father. As he gets ready to leave her in her room in Miss Minchin's school, he realizes how difficult the parting will be for Sara. He then brings out his third and last gift. It is the doll Emily, who he says has come all the way from France just to be with Sara. He tells Sara that dolls make the best of friends and that whatever she tells Emily, Emily will communicate to him. Sara believes him, and as she steps out of the room, she turns to take a quick look through the keyhole to see if Emily has moved.

Childhood: a Gift of the Imagination

Nostalgic constructions make their appearance only after the fact. However, the elements of the past that are evoked in these constructions indicate the dissatisfactions with the present. The nostalgia for childhood that is expressed in the 1995 *A Little Princess* is without doubt expressive of white male anxieties about the loss of empire and of authority over women. Yet the film also evokes one of the utopian elements of childhood, and that is the power of the imagination to counter the havoc wrought by war and capitalism. The film imagines the parent-child relationship as a spiritual and emotional one rather than a commercial one. It puts the gift of stories and the imagination in opposition to objects that can be bought in a mall. The parent-child bond it yearns for is one based on love, which lasts a lifetime and is not subject to the exchange values of the market.

A comparison of these three versions of *The Little Princess* shows that the romantic notion of childhood as an eternal state existing outside of history is untenable at the current moment, except when it is evoked nostalgically as a moment in history that is already lost to us. The girl child who was at the core of this idealization of children in general now appears to be an antique.

The aggressive invention of children as consumers—as agents who have to choose between a variety of goods available in the market and who no longer are guaranteed protections under law or public policy on account of their being children—makes it impossible to continue to show them as standing outside time. Rowan Williams, the archbishop of Canterbury, explains the long-term latency and protection granted to children by making the analogy between a society and a train: It is only a society that is confident of having the resources to carry passengers, of living alongside people whose participation in our social forms is not like ours, that can guarantee childhood. Our current society, according to Williams, is so focused on pushing children into adult or pseudoadult roles that it is quickly losing that kind of commitment.[20] There is little in Williams's account regarding how this loss of commitment is a specific historical outcome of the expansion of capitalism. Capital is not driven by human need but by the need to accumulate capital. Toward that purpose, it is completely logical that the boundaries around children be transgressed so as to bring children into the market, both as laborers and as consumers. In this scenario, to give a child the gift of imagination is to nurture her to withstand the impoverished human relations of capital, where each confronts the other as an antagonist.

3 | Of Cowboys and Indians

Hollywood's Games with History and Childhood

If, though, a modern poet maintains that there exists for each individual an image around which the entire world appears to founder [versinkt], for how many does that image not rise out of an old toy chest?

—Walter Benjamin

While there is a great deal of alarm over children's loss of innocence as it relates to adult secrets of sex, violence, and commerce, there is yet another, more crucial, element of the idea of childhood innocence that is being deconstructed almost without notice: the notion that children are innocent of history. In the classic conception of childhood as the empty space or the tabula rasa between the past and the future, children were imagined as simply inheriting the world they were born into with no responsibility for its inequities. For instance, we do not hold a white child responsible for white racism.

The notion that childhood is the site from which the present can be criticized and an alternative utopian future imagined is a product of the modernist conception of history as materialist, quite separate from myth and legend. A mythic understanding of history assumes that events are preordained and human beings are powerless to intervene in or change the course of events. A materialist conception, on the contrary, understands that historical events are the result of human action; it therefore also recognizes the possibility of breaking from the past. It is only upon the latter that the idea of childhood can be sustained. In a society that believes that people are destined to live in poverty or wealth according to their circumstance of birth, children are no different from adults and come with their fates predetermined. The feudal lord's son learns to be a lord, and the serf's son learns to be a serf. The idea that working-class children can change their class through education is premised upon the idea that new beginnings are possible through human agency. It is also premised upon universalism, the notion that as human beings we have some things in common, for example, we all want the best for our children.

The postmodern condition is marked, as both Fredric Jameson and Jurgen Habermas have suggested, by a loss of history and utopian ideas. It is manifested in the dystopian images of the future that abound in contemporary popular culture. Jameson explains that our inability to think historically manifests itself in the failure to see the present moment as part of history or as an outcome of history. This failure is a result of the commodification of history, such that the past is conjured up as a series of costumes or styles—for instance, as a kind of game between cowboys and Indians—with no allusion to the material conflicts that characterize earlier times and ours.[1]

Postmodern theory insists that there is no metanarrative of history, that there is only a plurality of little narratives, each valid in its own right. This view very much resonates with consumer culture. Capitalism, driven by the constant need to expand consumption, has to perpetuate a throwaway culture, one that has built into it disposability, temporariness, and obsolescence. Constant novelty in fashions, styles, and fads is an essential feature of consumer culture. Change, then, begins to be perceived as the defining feature of this way of being, a feature that finds its way into postmodern theory's refusal to seek any continuities or underlying explanations in history. The refusal to find any explanations for history is, as Jameson has suggested, part of the "structure of feeling" of late twentieth-century capitalism. It can be an outcome of being confronted by a world that seems to escape our grasp or a retreat from active political engagement with changing that world. It supports wild conspiracy theories about aliens or terrorists, the belief that technology has a life of its own independent of human agency, and a continued reliance on fate, destiny, or God as an explanation for the present.

In contrast, Marxist theory points to continuities in history: scarcity and class struggle. If patterns can be discerned in history, it is

possible to break away from it. In other words, you have to understand how something works if you want to fix it. The imagination to
think of an alternative can spring dialectically, as Eagleton clarifies,
only from the very same history. Childhood is perhaps among the most
ambitious projects to grow out of such an imagination. Marxists, however, are not the only ones who think that the present is connected to
both the future and the past, and not in an arbitrary, haphazard way.
Capitalists too look for continuities in time. Profits are calculated over
time. So are rates of interests and hourly wages. This is not to suggest
that either the capitalists or the socialists think the future can be pre-
dicted with accuracy. They agree that the outcome of any history is
not predetermined. Nevertheless, both seek to find explanations for
the outcome after the event.

If history is merely "a ceaseless chance twist of the kaleidoscope,"
to use Terry Eagleton's colorful summation of some postmodern thinking, it is impossible to predict the future or control it.[2] The chroni-
cler who recites events without distinguishing between the major and
minor ones, according to Walter Benjamin, does so in the belief that
nothing should be lost to history.[3] But it is only when all humankind
can make its own history that we can receive all our histories equally.
Until then, history is a contest, a narrative of the victors. Writing history, therefore, is an intensely political act, and only that historian can
spark a hope, Benjamin writing under the Nazis passionately advocated, who "is convinced that even the dead will not be safe from the
enemy if he wins. And the enemy has not ceased to be victorious."[4]
The danger now is that consumer culture threatens to erode that sense
of urgency from the retelling of history by reducing it to a costume
party. The dead, in this case, are erased from memory not by a totalitarian regime but by the mind-numbing tyranny of the market's demand that we should not take things too seriously.

The idea of childhood is inextricably connected to both a sense
of history and the utopian view that another world is possible. To see
a new beginning with the birth of a child assumes that it is possible
to change the present and act upon the future. This makes me ask:
Can childhood, whose symbolic value is so tied to a sense of history
and utopian ideas, survive their loss in the late twentieth century?

We can see the reinvention of the relationship between childhood,
history, and utopia in two Hollywood films made for children in the
1990s that explicitly address the historical relationship between Native Americans and the founding of the nation: *Pocahontas* (1996) and

Indian in the Cupboard (1996). Both films were produced in the five-hundredth year of Columbus's arrival and attempt to resolve the Native American experience of the founding of the nation as genocide with the "American dream" of progressive nationalism in which all gradually find their place. Both offer children's play to conjure up the past and in the process construct what it means to be a child.

Pocahontas—Disney's History Lesson for Children

Disney marketed the film *Pocahontas* as an American legend, a mix of myth, magic, and history. It is based on the history and legend of Pocahontas, who saved the life of John Smith, an Englishman captured by her father, by pleading with her father to show mercy and not kill him. On the basis of what records are available, the film is a distortion of history. Contrary to the young woman in love shown in the film, Pocahontas was only thirteen or fourteen when she saved John Smith, already in his forties. Karen Robertson, a historian, points out in "Pocahontas at the Masque" that Pocahontas was kidnapped by the British in 1613. when she was already married to Kokoum (who is presented as her suitor in the film) and kept hostage in Jamestown for a year. Here she was forcibly converted to Christianity and married John Rolfe, with none of the romantic involvement with John Smith shown in the film. Further, contrary to the film's happy ending in which Pocahontas chooses to stay with her people rather than follow John Smith, she was taken to England, where she was a curiosity and a showpiece for the empire. Subsequently, she gave birth to a child and died in England, never returning to Jamestown. Fabricating the myth of romantic love between John Smith and Pocahontas amounts to, as Robert Eaglestaff, a Native American activist, declared, "trying to teach about the Holocaust and putting in a nice story about Anne Frank falling in love with a German officer."[5]

While there is scant regard for history in the film, there is hardly any integrity toward the legend either. Disney adds an entirely new twist to the tale by transforming John Smith from the rescued into a heroic rescuer. John Smith, in fact, rescues twice. He first rescues a sailor from drowning on the way to America and then saves Pocahontas's father, Powhatan. Just after Pocahontas has stopped her father from killing John Smith, Ratcliffe, the English commander, fires at the unarmed Powhatan. John Smith then swings into action, comes between the bullet and Powhatan, and takes the injury upon himself.

As John D'Entremont writes in a review of the film for the *Journal of American History*, the Indians are transformed from a brave and proud people who chose to act with mercy by letting go an invader into a lucky people who owe the Englishman their life. In the final shot of the film, Powhatan comes laden with gifts to say goodbye to John Smith. "You are always welcome among my people," he tells Smith, whom he now calls "brother." The ravages of history are dissolved in this Hollywood closure, the oppressor now welcomed as brother. The legend, however, tells of another plea, lost in this filmic version. Powhatan reportedly warned Smith: "Take away your guns and your swords, the cause of all our jealousy, or you may all die in the same manner."[6]

At the time of the film's release, there was strong criticism by Native American groups, schoolteachers, individuals, and historians of its misrepresentation of history. Vivian Sobchack cited *Pocahontas* as another case of the commodification of history in the twentieth century, when "history has become a commodity—something to be 'fixed' according to maximum consumer desire, that is, not only made secure but also 'neutered,' 'altered,' and 'doctored up.'"[7] The film became a pretext for marketing consumer goods created around the Pocahontas theme. Reports noted the popularity of Jamestown, Virginia, particularly the museum, as a tourist site. Disney financed the floodlighting of St. James, the church in Gravesend, England, where Pocahontas lies buried, which also reported increased tourist visits. Finally, the plethora of commodities launched by Disney's lineup of tie-in merchandise ranged from activity and picture books, stuffed animals, and computer games to tie-ins with Burger King, Nestle's chocolates, and the like. The Pocahontas theme could be consumed without ever seeing the film, an example of what Susan Willis in *A Primer for Daily Living* has called "hyperconsumption."

History "for" Children

Seeing *Pocahontas* as simply another example of late twentieth-century capitalist cannibalization of history without attention to the film's positioning of itself as a history "for" children is an inadequate critique, both of the extent to which the film commodifies history and the commodification of all life, including childhood, in late capitalism. This view is unable to refute the widespread defense of the film that it was made for children and therefore not bound by history or legend but open to imaginative interpretation.

Nor can such a critique point to the poverty of the film's imagination regarding magic and childhood. A typical defense of the film, for example, called upon the reviewers to "lighten up" and see that the film was fiction and made for children.[8] Letters to editors from parents and teachers credited the film as a "fun way" to get children interested in history. Disney too disdained what it characterized as PC demands for faithfulness to history. James Pentecost, the film's producer, claimed: "Nobody should go to an animated cartoon hoping to get the accurate description of history."[9]

The film's narrative and its marketing both dismiss commitment to history as an "attitude," as a particularly oppressive adult way of thinking that suspects anything new. In the film's narrative, the unsmiling Kokoum, Pocahontas's suitor, embodies this. He remains wedded to his traditional role as a warrior, fighting first the other tribes and then the English. Even though in the course of the film we learn that the English are a new kind of enemy, both in appearance and weaponry, Kokoum's response does not move outside tradition, ritual, and repetition. Pocahontas rejects his proposal of marriage because, as she tells Grandmother Willow, he is "too serious." The supposed magic in the film is its reinvention of history by setting up a romance between John Smith and Pocahontas. Those who question the film's happy ending, Disney and others who defend the film seem to say, are, like Kokoum, just "too serious," unable to have fun with magic or animation.

However, magic is the least of the ingredients in this self-proclaimed mix of history, legend, and magic. Instead of playing with the magical qualities of animation to present its historical interpretation of what might have been, the film secures closure through the imitative realism of its form and happy ending. The transformative quality of animation lies in its ability to create something out of nothing, to stretch and pull, to defy the laws of physics and thus express an imagination that is not realistic. This quality was greatly admired by Eisenstein, who saw in the changeability and mobility of Disney's cartoons a rejection of U.S. standardization.[10]

Disney's animation has, however, with new technical innovations, such as 3-D animation in *Toy Story* and *Toy Story 2* (1995, 2000), progressively moved toward imitating live-action films rather than flout their rules. The animation in *Pocahontas* is strongly illusionist. In a reversal of the usual Disney anthropomorphizing, the animals do not talk—only squeal. The willow tree who is Pocahontas's confidante can

talk but is tied down to her roots. Even more startling is the natural-
ism with which the human form is represented. The Indians are all
presented as human, although without nipples. Several reviewers remarked on the natural tint of Pocahontas's skin, the agility and smooth-
ness of her movements. While she can dive off cliffs and swim
underwater, Hollywood's laws of continuity restrain her moves from
becoming unpredictable. Her long hair does sway somewhat wildly
with the wind. However, even the hair moves in a rather orderly fashion, as in shampoo commercials.

When it is naturalized (as opposed to magical or caricature), animation pushes to another level the commodification of human actors.
It can eliminate real human beings entirely by creating the ideal body
and face through an amalgamation of different types. This is clear from
the case of the model Dyna Taylor, who claimed that hers was the face
of Pocahontas in the film. Paid two hundred dollars in modeling fees,
Taylor received no screen credit because the studios claimed that they
had used several models to come up with the face of Pocahontas. The
explanation is certainly a plausible one. Nevertheless, it indicates that
animation is reduced to being another cost-cutting measure while dull-
ing its aesthetic possibilities. The animated figure that replaced the
child star is the manifestation of the postmodern loss of faith in an
authentic self, confirming the suspicion that beneath our faces is a computer microchip, a robot, or a cartoon character.

Rayna Green in "The Pocahontas Perplex" writes that between the
midsixteenth and the mideighteenth centuries, as the colonies moved
toward independence, the dominant stereotype of the Native American woman was transformed from a full-bodied, powerful, nurturing
but dangerous mother-goddess into a younger, leaner, princesslike figure. She was both Britannia's daughter and Caribbean queen, more in
the Caucasian mode even though her skin remained tinted. The film
never raises any of these other ghosts of Pocahontas. Instead,
Pocahontas is another incarnation of Barbie, the most circulated image of ideal feminine beauty for children.

Philip Young, in *The Mother of Us All*, also indicates that there
has always been a lewd side to the Pocahontas story. John Smith's account, for instance, describes Pocahontas coming naked out of the
woods: "All these nymphs tormented me more than ever, with crowd-
ing, pressing and hanging about, most tediously crying, Love you not
me?"[11] To portray Pocahontas realistically as a thirteen-year-old would
have made it difficult to sustain the myth of a romance between John

3.1. Pocahontas, an amalgamation of Barbie and an Asian model, is another addition to the ethnic Barbies, along with the Indian Barbie and the African Barbie.

Smith and Pocahontas. However, that threat is contained by presenting her as an adult woman in her most commodified form, the Barbie doll.

Magic is limited to the scenes of Native American magic making, such as the scene in which the wise man raises visions of the Englishmen from fire, Pocahontas's introduction of John Smith to the forest in the song "Colors of the Wind," and the caricatures of Ratcliffe and his sidekick. Pocahontas's sensuous relationship to nature is most strongly evoked as she sings, in "Colors of the Wind": "But if you walk the footsteps of a stranger, / You'll learn things you never knew you never knew." As the wind circles around her and Smith's heads, it changes both the shapes and colors of John Smith and Pocahontas, and we get a glimpse into another way of seeing.

There are hints here of what Benjamin saw as the power of fairy tales: their utopian imagery of the end of scarcity. In fairy tales, Benjamin pointed out, nature is always on the side of the little people who are able to shake off mythic explanations of the present as preordained:

The fairy tale tells us of the earliest arrangements that mankind made to shake off the nightmare which myth had placed upon its chest. In the figure of the fool it shows us how mankind "acts dumb" toward the myth; in the figure of the youngest brother it shows us how one's chances increase as the mythical primitive times are left behind; in the figure of the man who sets out to learn what fear is it shows us that the things we are afraid of can be seen through; in the figure of the wiseacre it shows us that the questions posed by the myth are simple minded, like the riddle of the Sphinx; in the shape of animals which come to the aid of the child in the fairy tale it shows that nature is not only subservient to the myth, but much prefers to be aligned with man. The wisest thing—so the fairy tale taught mankind in olden times, and teaches children to this day—is to meet the forces of the mythical world with cunning and with high spirits.[12]

The film, however, teaches no such lesson. Instead, it robs Pocahontas of the continued power she holds on the U.S. imagination about its national origins by putting her in the never-never land of "once upon a time," on which it slaps a happy ending. Here Disney follows its track record of domesticating fairy tales, as Jack Zipes has shown in *Breaking the Magic Spell*, by mass-producing them as spectacles of entertainment. Disney grants closure to this particular tale through the ideological certainty of nationalism and the sentimentalism of heterosexual romance. Here love transcends all barriers, including those of language and power. Grandmother Willow asks Pocahontas to listen with her heart. Pocahontas does exactly that and, after a hesitation of less than a minute, begins talking to John Smith in English at their very first meeting. The romantic love that develops between Pocahontas and John Smith transforms the relationship between Native Americans and their invaders into one of friendship. Ultimately, U.S. history becomes not one of conquest but of happy reconciliation between the conqueror and the conquered. This ideological closure makes Disney's rendering of history not utopian but revisionist.

In so cannibalizing history, Disney does not spare the notion of childhood. The studio's fabrication of history is justified on the basis of both a reinstatement of childhood and its ultimate trivialization. In the modernist imagery of childhood as innocent of history, children's play was the site from which new possibilities subversive of the status quo could be imagined, because children, not yet socialized into the inequities of history, were free to reinvent it, at least in play. The film invokes childhood to justify its play with a painful moment in U.S. history. Yet when challenged about their version, the film's producers insist that the audience should not take its interpretation too seriously. It is, after all, only child's play, they say. Child's play, here, is reduced to nothing more than the consumption of ninety minutes of "nonserious" fun with history in a darkened theater. This is an early lesson in accepting the tyrannical demand of the entertainment industry that we must enter its halls with our brains turned off. Contrast this to the utopian visions of alternative futures that Walter Benjamin saw arising out of toy chests in the quotation at the beginning of this chapter.

To use the concept of children's play to defend the film is to agree to Disney's reinvention of play as entertainment and thus reduce it from a site of utopian thinking to a site of consuming market-produced commodities. This is a serious reduction of the symbolic value of childhood. Of course, seriousness is hardly a desirable quality in the idealized consumer in late capitalism. In an economy run on debt, the adult consumer too is drawn in the image of the child—impulsive, seeking immediate gratification, and playfully consuming toys such as computers and cars. Accepting that history, and therefore the present, is just another source of fun and pleasure, and that no work is required for social transformation, is to shirk adult responsibility for acting in the present. It thus makes a pygmy of the adult at the same time it empties childhood of its distinction as a place from which another world can be imagined.

Indian in the Cupboard

The film *Indian in the Cupboard* at first glance appears to be a critique of the trivialization of history, utopia, and childhood in contemporary children's consumer culture, of which *Pocahontas* is a prime example. *Indian in the Cupboard*, like the version of *A Little Princess* released a year earlier, in 1995, responds nostalgically to the deconstruction of childhood, evoking it as a state different from adulthood, one that is almost spiritual but lost in the process of modernity. It attempts to imbue childhood with mystery, presenting it as a state with secrets that adults cannot enter. However, its nostalgia cannot escape the commodification of history and childhood that has become a general feature of children's consumer culture.

The film is based on the novel of the same title by Lynne Reid

3.2. A magic cupboard for big boys with money

Banks, who wrote a series of books in which Omri, a seven-year-old boy, confronts the past through his magic cupboard, which can bring contemporary plastic toys to life. Omri brings to life Little Bear, an Iroquois Indian from 1761, who has a profoundly transformative effect on him. He helps Omri make the transition from childhood into adolescence, from a shy, introverted child who learns to control his desires to consume into a responsible young man who is connected to his family and collective past.

The wish that the plastic toy should become a real person speaks of a deep longing for the human community so lacking in the solitary life of the bourgeois child left alone in a room full of toys. Brian Sutton-Smith in *Toys as Culture* has shown that since the Second World War there has been an unprecedented increase in the number of toys given to children, and that the primary function of toys since the war has been to socialize the child into being alone.

Omri is shown to be a particularly lonesome child. The film begins with a celebration of his seventh birthday. There is no big party, few presents, and Omri has only his immediate family and best friend, Patrick, along with Patrick's mother and brother, in attendance. He is a stranger even to his family, including his parents, who don't quite seem to know him. The youngest of three boys, Omri seems unable to "grow up" and cope with the world outside the home. His lack of appetite, fear of the dark, inability to go out alone, and shyness in school all indicate his isolation.

Little Bear enriches Omri's life by becoming alternately child, friend, and ultimately parent. Physically a giant in comparison with the miniature Little Bear, Omri starts off by assuming the role of a parent to him. He takes care of Little Bear's needs, providing him with food and material to build a tepee, and protects him from the guinea pig that his brothers keep. "Having him," Omri tells his best friend, Patrick, is "like having a child." When on the insistence of Patrick, Omri brings to life a cowboy, Boo-hoo Boone, he also has to intervene in the incessant fighting between Little Bear and Boo. Here the Native American experience of history as a struggle is trivialized into a children's game of cowboys and Indians. Little Bear and Boo call each other names and tease each other. In a clever play on the stereotyped image of children as unthinking mimics who will be violent if they see violence, Little Bear and Boo are transformed into children as they begin to fight while watching an old Western on television. Patrick and Omri, on the other hand, appear adultlike as, with a remote in hand, they sit indifferent to the violence on the screen, knowing it is not true but only an image.

The backward projection of Little Bear and Boo as childlike is important to the plot, in that it shows the transformation of Omri from a pseudoadult into a child. However, it also reduces Native American struggles to children's games. Miniaturizing the historical conflict in this way suggests that its outcomes are not present with us now, that it is a part of our history that is of no use in the present. The process is similar to what happens when adult things are miniaturized, for example, teacups and trains; no longer functional, they become playthings.

As the narrative develops, Little Bear transitions from being a child into being Omri's companion. He enables Omri to separate from his mother, to be alone in a room with the door shut and the light off, and to come out of the shadow of his elder brothers. But most important of all, Little Bear finally becomes Omri's adult friend and helps initiate him into manhood. The film expresses a deep nostalgia for adult men like Little Bear who can take the initiation of the young into their hands and teach children about the traditions and history of their community. Neither of the men in Omri's life, his teacher or his father, seem able to understand the profound transformation that he is undergoing. The teacher, although well meaning, remains outside Omri's emotional life. For a class project, Omri tells of his adventures with Little Bear, which the teacher indulgently dismisses as no more than his "imagination." The father, although caring, remains distant. He is taken aback at the vehemence with which Omri insists that he is now old enough to go alone to the corner store.

Omri's tumultuous growing up happens unknown to these adult men. In contrast, Little Bear had been fully occupied with initiating his nephew into adulthood, taking him to the edge of the woods on a coming-of-age journey, when Omri pulled him into the present through his magic cupboard. Little Bear now continues that lesson with Omri, teaching him first about Iroquois tradition but ultimately about being brave and surviving. Most of all, Little Bear teaches Omri about death. In one sequence, Omri, carried away by the power of his magic cupboard, brings to life an old chief whose weapons he wants for Little Bear. The chief, however, dies of shock. Completely stunned by the awesome consequences of his actions, Omri wants to turn the chief back into plastic. Little Bear, however, insists on the dignity of a ritual burial.

This is a turning point in the film: Omri becomes a child in relation to Little Bear. Before leaving the room to go meet his father, he asks Little Bear, "Are you mad at me?" "You really are a child," replies Little Bear, looking back at him in pity. At the end of the film, the relationship between Little Bear and Omri is finally transformed, with Little Bear physically an adult and Omri a young man on the threshold of adulthood. Little Bear, no longer a miniature, stands tall before the admiring gaze of Omri, who is now a child by comparison. Persistent racism, however, forecloses the possibility of Little Bear's displacing the father. He is at best an equal, mostly an uncle. This is best represented in the scene where Little Bear is building his log house in Omri's room while the father is working in the garage. Their hammering echoes in harmony, with Little Bear's making the gentler sound. At the end of the film, Little Bear adopts Omri as a nephew, not a son. This white child of the late twentieth century cannot change these historical hierarchies even in his imaginative life.

The Magic Cupboard and the Rejection of Consumer Culture

The film's rejection of the commodification of children's culture is manifested in its disdain for plastic. Plastic has, as Susan Willis suggests in *A Primer for Daily Living*, come to epitomize mass-produced, homogeneous, disposable commodity culture. Used as packaging, it is also the most useless part of the commodity, to be thrown away. Plastic toys have become emblematic of mass-produced consumer culture and considered inauthentic, robbing children of direct contact with the real. This explains Roland Barthes's contention that "current toys are made of graceless material, the product of chemistry, not nature. Many are now molded from complicated mixtures; the plastic material of which they are made has an appearance at once gross and hygienic, it destroys all the pleasure, the sweetness, the humanity of touch. A sign which fills one with consternation is the gradual disappearance of wood, in spite of its being an ideal material because of its firmness and its softness, and the natural warmth of its touch; . . . wood makes essential objects, objects for all time."[13] There is undoubtedly, as Ellen Seiter has pointed out in *Sold Separately*, a class bias against plastic toys on account of their low market value, which makes them, by necessity, the toys that working-class children play with. The cheapest toys in the market, doled out as tie-ins with chains like McDonald's and Burger King, they have no value as cultural capital. Consequently, they are the most expendable item of the bourgeois playroom. The rejection of the plastic toy is completely consistent with *Indian in the Cupboard*'s validation of the middle-class heterosexual family, with a stay-at-home mother as a prerequisite for reinstating childhood.

In holding up the toy figurine of the Native American as the toy with a soul as opposed to the more contemporary children's toys, the film expresses deep nostalgia for the toys that parents themselves knew as children, and consequently for a connection with the nation's history. Contemporary children's plastic toys in the film are seen as introducing children to violent themes and thus vitiating children's games. When Omri puts his collection of Power Rangers, GI Joes, and dinosaurs in his cupboard, he is terrified at their mutation into real. They spew fire and point their lasers at him, threatening to destroy both him and the cupboard.

This brief scene comes close to another genre of films based on children's toys: the adult horror film in which children's toys embody evil, as part of either satanic rites or capitalist greed. In the film series *Child's Play* (1991, 1993, 1994), the demonic spirit of a child killer possesses Chucky, a doll who then goes on a killing spree. The manufacturers of Chucky are presented as ruthless, profit-hungry business-men who relaunch the doll despite knowing its earlier history. This in-dicates adult anxieties around corporations' taking over their children's souls, turning them into monsters the parents have no control over.

The desire for the "simple" toy of the past is a nostalgic desire for the simple child whom the parent knew and understood. In the film's narrative, investing plastic toys with lives from the past becomes a means to restore the sacred to children's toys and to bring back mys-tery into the playroom. Children are invoked as mediums through whom the past can be restored. The past, in the film, is like a shadow that lies under the present, with lessons for the present that have been forgotten. In the opening scene, the camera pulls out of a miniature Indian village model built by the children, which dissolves into a shot of the school playground.

The magic of the cupboard is premised upon its being old and devoid of commercial value. It is an antique-looking piece found by Omri's brother among the trash. The key that unlocks the cupboard comes out of Omri's mother's collection of keys that have no functional purpose. It was the key his mother had asked of her grandmother, who on her deathbed had nothing of value to give her. That key symbol-izes an aspect of the mother's childhood that she had forgotten but one that she unknowingly passes on to her child: the ability to find meaning in the rejects of adult society.

There is a profound sense here of Benjamin's theory that children were scavengers or trash collectors; not yet socialized into valuing things by their market value, he argued, children could invest junk with new meaning. Similarly, children have no patience with the adult instruction that they "play carefully" with expensive toys or keep them as objects of display. Chiding child psychologists for an unnecessary infatuation with producing objects for children, Benjamin stated that "the world is full of the most unrivalled objects for childish attention and use. . . . In waste products children recognize the face that the world of things turns directly and solely to them. In using these things they do not so much imitate the works of adults as bring together in the artifact produced in play, materials of widely differing kinds in a new, intuitive relationship. Children thus produce their own small world of things within the greater one."[14]

The magic cupboard connects Omri to both his family history and a more collective history. In coming to know the past as a living entity,

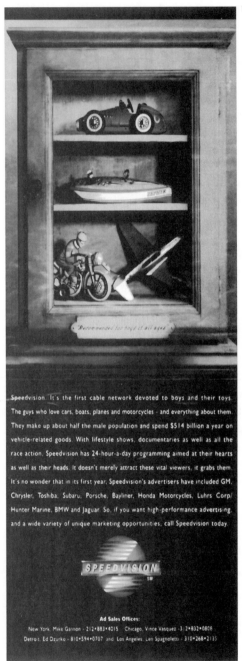

3.3. The magic ends and the sale begins.

he reacts strongly to its diminution into a style or fashion. In one sequence, a boy sporting an Indian hairstyle accosts Omri in the street and forcibly takes away his money. Omri shouts after him, "You don't deserve that hair." On the sound track is Little Bear chanting the funeral rites for the old chief whom Omri had brought to life. Confronted with a present in which the past is no more than a "style" and a child just beginning to comprehend death, Little Bear's chants indicate a profound loss of history, one in which the dead must mourn their own demise.

The film presents children's consumer culture as vacuous and even frightening to children. It is seen as putting pressure on children to assume responsibility for choices whose consequences they cannot understand. Although Omri is empowered by his ability to transform his toys into real people—initially, he is the master of his playroom— he finds himself unable to deal with the consequences of his actions. Besides causing the death of an old chief, Omri ends up losing the key to the cupboard. Both Little Bear and Boo face the dismal possibility of a life as miniatures, forever dependent on their child masters for survival. To Boo's panic-stricken call, "Oh God!" Little Bear replies, "There is no God here, only children." The film obtains closure by transforming Omri into a child under the guidance of an adult. In a definite late twentieth-century twist to the classic fairy tale—which, as Bruno Bettelheim pointed out in *The Uses of Enchantment*, typically ended with the child protagonist returning home—an adult, Omri, lost amidst the isolation and bewildering responsibilities imposed by consumer culture, returns home a child.

The film's nostalgia for the possibilities of new beginnings embodied in childhood shows itself in the adoring gaze with which it holds up the child as a spectacle. The first time that Omri hears sounds from the cupboard and leaves his bed to open the cupboard, he is transformed. The sound track with its operatic music emphasizes the spectacle. An extreme close-up of his feet exaggerates his size. Even before he has opened the cupboard, Omri is a giant compared to the little Indian he will find hiding inside. Another extreme close-up on his hands and the key continues to exaggerate Omri's size. Little Bear asks, "Are you a giant"? "Who me? I am a boy," replies Omri. His face fills the whole screen, but it is the face of a child excited at the awesome possibility of his toy coming to life. "The great white spirit can be a child," says Little Bear. Children are seen as redeemers of the past.

Both Little Bear and Boo express a longing for children, saying that "children help you heal."

Yet the film also recognizes that not all losses can be redeemed. Before entering the magic cupboard for the last time and being transported back to his own time, Little Bear asks Omri if the Onandaga are always a great people. Standing in the future and knowing what Little Bear does not yet know, Omri replies that the Onandaga are always a great people, but "things are not always so good." This is the single moment in the film when the present and the past are connected in a dialogue. It is also the moment that the child is represented as the inheritor of an alternative future that is built upon the redemption of past inequities.

However, this site of action is contained as Little Bear steps back into the old cupboard, never to bother Omri with questions regarding the present again. The film presumes that the Onandaga have been absorbed into history and no longer live as Omri's contemporaries. Native Americans are assumed to be part of America's past, literally outside time, the trick by which, as Johannes Fabian in *Time and the Other* has pointed out, the other is produced. In its attempt to suggest that Omri now lives in a multiracial America in which racial conflicts are resolved, an Indian boy is cast as Omri's best friend. He is, however, not an American Indian but from India, presumably born and raised in the United States—a farcical repetition of Columbus's mistake.

By Way of a Conclusion

Pocahontas and *Indian in the Cupboard* appear to be opposing responses in their textual strategies to the contemporary crisis over the loss of childhood innocence. *Pocahontas* interprets children's relationship to history as one of playful consumption. The text, in form (naturalistic animation and closed narrative) and content (ideological certainty of heterosexual romance and nationalism), is neither open-ended nor playful in raising the possibility of what might have been. Children's play with history is thus literally reduced to consuming commodities—toys, clothes, foods, locations—branded with the Pocahontas "theme."

Indian in the Cupboard seems a direct rejection of exactly this kind of commodification of history for children. Omri learns to value the past as a living, breathing entity with lessons for the present rather than as a commodity to be played with and then discarded. Omri learns that reducing the bitter conflicts of the past to plastic toys and hair-styles is a travesty. The film restores the notion that children, not yet socialized into the inequitable relations of their society, have the po-tential to heal it. Play with the past becomes in this film a way by which the child learns to grow up and face the challenges of life. The film also redefines play, not as consumption but as a tactile relation-ship with the world in which Omri learns about the Native American way of life by having a close relationship with Little Bear and learn-ing from him.

However, both films end up on the market shelves of children's consumer culture by placing Native Americans in the land of "once upon a time." Consequently, the ongoing struggles of Native Ameri-cans are shoved outside history and turned into objects of entertain-ment in the present. This justifies Disney's "playful" rendering of history and *Indian in the Cupboard*'s happy ending. Both give ideo-logical justification to the notion of the American dream: that conflicts are ultimately resolved and harmony restored, as different groups in-evitably move up and join the nation—so much so that past conflicts can now be told as fairy tales to children.

The genie in *Aladdin* (1992), another Disney film, sings of a "whole new world" that is free of history. This freedom from history in the late twentieth century is the freedom of the marketplace, where seg-ments of the past sit on the shelves equally and we can choose our own versions with no consequences. Further, regardless of the pro-tests in *Indian in the Cupboard* against "playing" with history, and its nostalgia for children's play as sacred and filled with mystery, the video version of the film came with "your own cupboard, key and In-dian." Like *Pocahontas*, *Indian in the Cupboard* generated the trash-ing of history that its text tried so hard to salvage.

Childhood, no longer an essential attribute of the child, becomes, as the Disney promotions would have it, "an attitude" available to any adult or child with the money to buy it. The admonition to not be "too serious" stares down at us, from the market shelves and the movie theaters to postmodern theory's rejection of underlying explanations. Contrast Benjamin's toy chest that begins this chapter with the toy chest in a print advertisement run by SpeedVision, a television channel that sells its audience of upscale men to marketers in *Marketing Age*. The cupboard in this advertisement looks like Omri's magic cupboard. But instead of unleashing a break from history, this toy chest asks bourgeois men to indulge themselves, have fun, and buy more toys. While for Walter Benjamin work would become like child's play, a non-alienated activity, the best that the market can offer is alienated consumption of market-produced commodities. In the market, to play is to consume rather than to produce, to absorb rather than to invent, and finally to be an object rather than to be the subject of history.

4

Obsolescence and Other Playroom Anxieties

Toy Stories over a Century of Capital

Here are three narratives "for children," the first from the early twentieth century and the latter two from the last decade, each imagining a scenario in which toys come to life. From Margery Williams's *The Velveteen Rabbit or How Toys Become Real*:

> Only when a child loves you for a long, long time, not just to play with, but REALLY loves you, then you become real."

From the official Beanie Babies web page, July 10, 1996:

> NEWSFLASH . . . NEWSFLASH!!!
> Following are the Beanie Babies that are retiring this Mother's Day. Please take a few minutes to thank them for their years of service! . . .
> Flash the Dolphin
> Date of Birth—May 13th, 1993 [the oldest]
> Sparky the Dalmatian
> Date of Birth—February 27, 1996 [the youngest]

And from *Toy Story* (1995):

> We do not like being blown up, Sid, . . . or smacked or ripped apart. That's right. Your toys. Take care of your toys. Because

if you don't, we'll find out, Sid. We toys can see everything.
So *play nice.*

In these moments of transformation lie buried the cultural conception
of what it means to be human, not commodity; subject, not object;
agent, not another's plaything, and adult, not child. In other words,
these narratives ask the question, Is a nonalienated life possible? Since
the stories we tell children, as Jacqueline Rose has indicated in *The
Case of Peter Pan*, tell us more about adults' conception of childhood
than about children's experience of it, the shifting meaning of the toy
can reveal to us not only how we seek to socialize children into capitalism, but also how capital has transformed the very meaning of childhood over the course of a century.

The toy, insofar as it has been transformed into a commodity—
that is, it has an exchange value in the market—is, to paraphrase Marx,
"a very queer thing" that appears "at first sight, a very trivial thing,
and easily understood" but is in fact "abounding in metaphysical
subtleties and theological niceties."[1] It is both a commodity and an
analogy for commodified labor. In fact, the analogy between the mechanical toy and alienated labor was commonplace in the nineteenth
century, taken over by Marx when he described "the fully formed proletariat" as a "completed abstraction from everything human, even from
the appearance of being human."[2] The industrial proletariat, like the
mechanical toy, seemed condemned to performing mechanized, fragmented, and repetitive movements set to a relentless pace completely
outside its control, existing merely to make profits for others.

The metaphysical subtleties that surround commodities, according to Marx, relate to the fundamental question of who creates value.
It is labor—the only living element among others such as raw materials, capital, and land—Marx argued, that created value by transforming capital and raw material into commodities that were of use and
could also fetch a price on the market. For instance, neither capital
nor leather is capable on its own of making a pair of shoes. Profit, Marx
clarified, was the difference between the exchange value of labor (the
wages paid to labor) and the value that labor created (the market price
of commodities). The trick that capitalist ideology plays is to suppress
the fact that it is labor that creates value. Instead, it proclaims dead
labor—that is, capital (value created by labor that is accumulated as
profit)—as the creative force in production and represents this relationship between capital and labor as natural.

One of the main objectives of Marxist criticism, then, has been to uncover this ideological mystification of labor and class in popular cultural texts, including its internalization by our unconscious. Fredric Jameson's explanation in *The Political Unconscious* of how class and subjectivity in capitalism are reproduced in the unconscious is a productive approach to unraveling how popular children's narratives socialize children into capitalism. The stories we tell children about the meaning of toys and the proper way to relate with them contain lessons about being both workers and consumers.

However, attributing ideological meanings to toys comes up against their assumed innocence. As children's playthings, toys have acquired the aura of innocence associated with children, who were a century ago imagined to be the spiritual center of the bourgeois family. Presenting the home as a respite from the cruel world outside implicitly accepted the exploitation that existed "out there," making children terribly dependent upon the family for their sheer survival.

Contrary to the nineteenth-century myth that children were free from economics, their lives were inextricably tied to their parents' class status. Moreover, it was not until the early decades of the twentieth century that the idealized childhood free from labor was materially possible even for the bourgeois child. It was only in 1938 that the U.S. Congress passed the Fair Labor Standards Act, prohibiting child labor entirely. Charles Dickens's world of the streets, filled with the hardships of the working child, was right outside the bourgeois home and the fictions that supported it. The anxiety of losing the protection of one's parents and being turned onto the streets abounds in bourgeois children's fiction. For instance, Sara Crewe, the protagonist of Burnett's *Little Princess*, written in 1905, finds herself transformed into a scullery maid when her father is reported dead on the battlefield. Such romanticized fictions of childhood served to repress, diminish, and disavow the harsh economic and historical divisions of the outside world of which all, including children, were a part.

Inevitably, like all repressions, these childhood anxieties about loss of class privilege refused to be laid to rest but haunted the playroom in the figures of toys that come to life. Narratives about toys coming to life have been previously explained in terms of psychoanalytic narratives of the family. Mark Poster has convincingly argued in *Critical Theory of the Family* that the language of love and need used to describe children's relationship to toys—for example, the toy's desire to be loved by the child—reflects the extreme dependence of the child on the parent within the privatized bourgeois home. Similarly, Poster attributes the mystery surrounding toys' behavior when they come to life, usually at night, to the distance between the adult and the child and the inaccessibility of the parental world for the child. I take a different tack here, suggesting that the language of love and need ascribed to toys is also a response to the alienated relations of capitalism, and that these changing narratives about toys speak of an increasing expansion of capitalism into all areas of human life.

Toys, Childhood Innocence, and Industrial Capitalism

At the center of Margery Williams's 1922 children's story *The Velveteen Rabbit* is a toy rabbit in a little boy's nursery whose deepest desire is to turn into a real rabbit. He is mortified by feelings of inadequacy in comparison to the more "modern" mechanical toys in the nursery, who "pretended they were real because they could move."[3] These feelings speak of the anxieties of being made obsolete by other, more skilled, workers or by technology. The rabbit is also aware that he is imminently susceptible to being thrown into the trash heap. In other words, he knows that as a commodity he is disposable, and that only the boy's love can save him.

Williams depicts the rabbit's desire to become real with such sympathy that its temporary resolution in the middle of the story comes as a relief. For a while, the rabbit becomes the boy's favorite toy and so comes to believe that it is real. To carry off this narrative conceit, Williams has to rely on the cultural conception of childhood as distinct from adulthood and therefore casts the nursery as a special, mysterious world, giving it an almost religious sanctity. The Skin Horse, the oldest toy in the nursery, tells Rabbit about "nursery magic," which, the narrator tells us, "is very strange and wonderful, and only those playthings that are old and wise and experienced like the Skin Horse understand all about it. Only when a child loves you for a long, long time, not just to play with, but REALLY loves you, then you become real. . . . "It doesn't happen all at once," said the Skin Horse. "You become. It takes a long time. . . . Generally, by the time you are Real, most of your hair has been loved off, and your eyes drop out and you get loose in the joints and very shabby" (4–5). Unknown to the adults, the nursery is a secret enclave in which the boy and the rabbit share an intense friendship marked by "splendid games together, in whispers, when Nana had gone away to her supper and left the night-light burning on the mantelpiece" (9).

In this narrative, granting human feelings to the toy serves as a lesson to children about forming lasting relationships and is also a protest against the instrumental use of others. Williams dwells at length on the acute desire of Rabbit to become real. Even after he has obtained the boy's love, the rabbit continues to be plagued by self-doubt. One day he sees some real rabbits, who tell him that he smells of sawdust. The low point for the rabbit, however, is reached when Nana throws him in the trash when she cleans the boy's room after his recovery from scarlet fever. Forgotten by both the boy and the other toys, Rabbit lay in the trash, and

> a tear, a real tear, trickled down his little shabby velvet nose and fell to the ground. . . . Where the tear had fallen a flower grew out of the ground, a mysterious flower, not like any that grew in the garden, . . . and out of it there stepped a fairy. . . .
>
> "I am the nursery magic Fairy," she said. "I take care of all the playthings that the children have loved. When they are old and worn out, and the children don't need them anymore, then I come and take them away with me and turn them into Real."
>
> "Wasn't I Real before?" asked the little Rabbit.
>
> "You were Real to the Boy," the Fairy said, "because he loved you. Now you shall be Real to everyone." (23)

The fairy makes the rabbit real, with hind legs and all, and he comes to live with a bunch of real rabbits "forever and ever." The utopian fairy-tale ending wipes away the humiliations of being a disposable commodity and transforms the rabbit into an agent who lives in a community with other rejects of consumer culture. What better heaven could be imagined in capitalism?

Children's literature in the late nineteenth and early twentieth centuries could rely on the commonly accepted notion of childhood as an enclave not yet colonized by capital to invert its relationships in the playroom. For instance, in Carlo Collodi's *Adventures of Pinocchio*, when Pinocchio arrived in Playland, he found a country quite unlike any other. The population was composed entirely of boys; the oldest were fourteen and the youngest scarcely eight years old. The streets were filled with merriment, noise, and shouting. In this world, every day was a holiday; the autumn holiday began on the first day of January and ended on the last day of December. (The basic premise of Marx's "realm of freedom" was the shortening of the workday.)[4]

In Williams's tale, the evocation of childhood as innocent of commerce wrestles with a growing market in commodities produced for children. By the time *The Velveteen Rabbit* was written, children's literature, like children's clothes, furniture, and toys, was part of a growing market in children's consumer goods that invited the adult to buy these as gifts for a child. It speaks of Williams's insight that she casts the boy as a fickle consumer. Surrounded by a room filled with toys, he comes to love the rabbit just as easily (his Nana, one night, not finding his usual toy, hands him the rabbit) as he eventually abandons it. From the point of view of the rabbit/worker, it is no different from being arbitrarily chosen by a consumer/employer from a toy shelf lined with other mass-produced commodities/labor.

Moreover, Williams gives neither the boy nor the rabbit proper names. They are simply called Boy and Rabbit. This is quite a departure from the romantic celebration of the child as standing outside consumer culture. The idealized child in this case recognizes the intrinsic value of people and things over their exchange value. In Frances Hodgson Burnett's *Little Princess,* the child protagonist, Sara, remains listless and indifferent to the shopping spree organized by her father until she sees a particular doll in a shop window. Upon seeing this doll, Sara "recognizes" her to be Emily, a doll she had always dreamed of having. Sara is not interested in comparing prices and cannot—because of the stage of children's consumer culture in the late nineteenth century—ask for dolls by their brand names. The loss of proper names in Williams's story speaks to the homogenization imposed by the role of the consumer. The consumer-commodity relationship is necessarily a homogenizing one: One can replace the other, since all can be measured by one standard, money.

Late Twentieth-Century Toy Stories

By the end of the twentieth century, toy narratives were bringing down all the walls between the playroom and the market, parodying the notion that the playroom is a protected enclave. The plot of Disney's 1995 film *Toy Story* revolves around the rivalry between Woody, a toy cowboy, and Buzz Lightyear, the more mechanically endowed space ranger. Both of them belong to a boy called Andy, who is seven or eight years old and lives in a large suburban home with his mother and sister. The rivalry between Woody and Buzz leads them into being captured by Andy's neighbor, Sid, who is the bad child in the film. Woody and Buzz succeed in outwitting Sid and return home to Andy's playroom. Their rivalry is resolved with Buzz's final acceptance that he is not a real space ranger but a toy. Meanwhile, the toys have also taught Sid a lesson about not messing with toys but playing with them according to directions on the box.

The fear of obsolescence runs rampant in *Toy Story*. Not only do the toys fear being ousted from the child's nursery by the newer, more mechanically endowed toys, but also they dread being thrown in the trash or sold at the garage sale that follows every birthday and Christmas. The increased mobility of late capitalism makes matters even worse. In the opening sequence of the film, the toys in Andy's playroom are twice threatened: Andy's mother has decided to celebrate his birthday just before they move to a new place.

Toy Story, however, makes no attempt at evoking sympathy for the toys' anxieties. In contrast to the whispering toys of Williams's nursery who believed in magic, these cynical and jaded postmodern toys have no patience with the language of love and need. Unlike the rabbit who yearned for the boy's love, these toys accept as matter-of-fact that being a toy is no more than a job, with no love lost between the child and his toys. They go about doing their job, that is, *letting* children play with them, either good-naturedly, as in the case of Woody, or grudgingly, as in the case of Mr. Potato Head, who would rather find a Mrs. Potato Head and live on a couch. In spite of the centrality in the plot of the rivalry between Buzz and Woody for Andy's attention, the toys seem happiest when left alone. The Magna Doodle toy draws by itself, the tape recorder can display its messages, and Woody uses the remote car to tip off Buzz to Sid's backyard. Once Andy is out of the playroom, the toys organize themselves into a staff meeting with Woody at the head. They talk practically about dealing with plastic corrosion and the impending move. All they want is to avoid losing their jobs by being fired/thrown into the trash or deskilled/sold at a garage sale—while not having any particular love for their jobs, either.

There is, however, one toy, Buzz Lightyear, who thinks that he is real. The central conflict in the film's narrative revolves around making Buzz give up this delusion and accept that he is a toy. Much to the other toys' bemusement, Buzz insists that he is not a toy. Upon arriving in Andy's room, he gets busy sending signals to his space commander, refuses to take off his headgear (claiming he would die if he breathed the air), and boasts that he can fly. The other toys, however, check Buzz out as the latest entrant to a lower- or middle-level job. "I'm so glad you are not a dinosaur," says the dinosaur. "I just can't take that kind of rejection." The conversation that follows includes these lines: "Do you have copper wiring?" "Are you from Singapore? Hong Kong? I'm from Mattel—or actually, I am from a smaller company that was purchased and leveraged by Mattel." "I am from Playskool." Seeing Woody's obvious distress at the technological superiority of Buzz, Mr. Potato Head murmurs that Woody must have "laser envy."

Why do these lines evoke laughter from both adults and children in the audience? Poor Buzz, the most technologically superior toy, is actually an anachronism in this late twentieth-century playroom. He is quite simply from another century, when toys or people could talk about the possibility of a nonalienated life and children's playrooms were imagined as the opposite of the adult world. Mr. Potato Head's jibe at Woody's laser envy is a crack at psychoanalysis, which in the popular conception is viewed as a theory preoccupied with seeing childhood as the root of one's problems in life, giving childhood a significance that these toys have no patience for. For them, childhood is a nuisance and children no different from any other kind of bosses/consumers. Mr. Potato Head's desire to find Mrs. Potato Head, no more and no less, further pokes fun at the idea that the playroom is filled with ideas subversive to the status quo.

In its utopian (not romantic) versions, childhood was a call for, Adam Phillips suggests, "an alternative to passive acceptance."[5] The fundamental question for Freud, Phillips writes, was how people over the course of their lives lost their curiosity about life and their passionate love for it. Freud considered children's preoccupation with questions about sexuality, their bodies, and the adult world the manifestation of a passionate engagement with the world. Killing children's curiosity about sexuality to maintain "good behavior" induced, in Freud's view, "the neurosis that arises in unanswered questions—obsessive speculating."[6] Like Marx, Freud recognized the alienated life. The notion of the unconscious underlies the existence of inner conflicts, of what Phillips calls "other minds inside us" making us as "separate from ourselves as we are from other people."[7] The assumption shared by Marxist critiques of the ideology and the historical and material versions of psychoanalysis is that we can uncover and understand these other minds, act on the basis of such an understanding, and therefore act autonomously to change the social conditions that produce alienation. Childhood, Marxism, and psychoanalysis, all grounded in the nineteenth century, are united by their hope for the possibility of the nonalienated life.

However, in this postmodern playroom there is only one child, and that is Buzz. He wants the impossible. Like a child, he believes the world can be what he wants it to be. The narrative then sets out to convince him otherwise. Buzz realizes he is a toy when he sees himself advertised in a television commercial. He learns that he is one among multiple copies, his lines are pre-scripted, he cannot fly, and he comes with parts "sold separately." While the velveteen rabbit had learnt that it was not real by seeing real rabbits, Buzz realizes the same by seeing other market-produced commodities. Over a century of capitalism, its dominant narratives suggest that the possibility of a nonalienated life is a childish dream we have to be cured of.

There is a brief moment of sympathy for Buzz when he finds out that he is no more than a toy. The camera pulls back to the strains of "I'll Go Sailing No More," and we look down upon Buzz lying on the floor with a broken arm by his side. He now has lost all desire to find his way home. When Woody tries to convince him of Andy's need for him, Buzz asks with stunning clarity, "Andy's house or Sid's house— what is the difference?"

Toward its end, the film makes another faint-hearted gesture toward the power of the imagination and the desire to break out of prescripted definitions of the self. Buzz and Woody defy the television commercials and manage to fly. They light the rocket Sid had strapped on Buzz's back and land right in Andy's car. However, the resolution is distinctly nonclimactic. In the last scene, Buzz has accepted his status as a commodity and waits anxiously but sportingly with the other toys to hear what new toys Andy will acquire at Christmas. That we smile rather than cry at Buzz's falling in line is a narrative achievement made possible by the film's complete lack of nostalgia about the loss of childhood.

In deconstructing childhood, *Toy Story* tears down the walls around the playroom as well. In the romantic celebration of childhood, the playroom was surrounded in secrecy and mystery and its transgression into the rest of the house was a cause for alarm. In contrast, in *Toy Story* the whole house, designed in pastels like a plastic dollhouse, is itself a playroom. In one of *Toy Story*'s cleverest sequences, the toys come down from the playroom to check on the presents Andy receives on his birthday. The toy soldiers' adventures, edited perfectly to the conventions of the adult war genre, evoke toy commercials rather than any breaking of taboos.

Moreover, this generic house has no photographs or art that would make it unique or reflective of the people who live in it. We never see any work being done in the house. We see no kitchen, for example, which is such a center of life in the 1994 film *Little Women*. We also see no bedrooms other than Andy's, which is in fact more the toys' room than his. We see no attics, gardens, or even scary basements to hide in. In contemporary nostalgic representations, the home is cast as a sanctuary. In the 1995 *Little Princess*, for example, the last time we see Sara and her father together, Sara's bedroom is infused with a golden light and filled with a lush abundance of colors and fabrics, an abundance not restored until the end of the film when Sara is transformed into a princess again. The camera stands respectfully at a distance before moving in very slowly to show the father and daughter talking. Likewise, in *Little Women* the camera is often positioned as a window into the golden world of the family before it enters its intimate circle.

If the home is not a haven from the world in *Toy Story*, the children occupying it are not angelic innocents either. *Toy Story* parts ways with the typical thirties' children's film's adoring gaze upon the child. Instead, even babies like Andy's sister appear to be drooling imbeciles. The protagonist, Andy, is a bland, unimaginative little boy who plays clichéd cops-and-robbers games that the toys put up with. He also leads a remarkably isolated life. None of the large number of children who come to his birthday with presents show up to say goodbye when he moves out of his old house. Andy simply says, "Goodbye, house," and gets into the car with his mother. A large truck with their belongings, including his toys, follows them.

It is Sid, the bad boy, who, although just as isolated as Andy, is invested with some personality. However, he too is a parody. Called "Psycho" by the toys, he is a takeoff on the evil, satanic child of the adult horror-film genre. At one point in the film, Sid tortures Woody by burning him with a reflection through a magnifying glass. This is followed by a reverse shot of Sid's braces in an extreme close-up. This exaggerates his childishness, making us laugh at him rather than recoil in horror. Demystifying childhood as a mere irritant and a nuisance washes away the idea either that it is a blank slate that can be possessed by evil or that it is inherently good.

If grand ideas about some essential purity of children are dismissed in *Toy Story*, adulthood is not spared either. When the toys come to life, they act like routine-bound diminutive adults rather than mysterious, cruel, or powerful people. Petty middle managers rather than proud workers, they go about their daily routines, working out and polishing and servicing their parts so that they can continue to perform the tasks assigned to them.

That both children and adults in the audience laugh at this shrinking of adulthood can indicate the passing away of childhood and its more oppressive features: the terrible economic and emotional dependency of children upon adults, the deliberate killing of children's curiosity, their forced ignorance of sex and economics, and the voluntary withdrawal from spontaneity and play demanded of adulthood. *Toy Story*'s children lead remarkably autonomous lives within the family. Andy lives alone with his mother and sister, and we never even see Sid's parents. Mostly out of the children's lives, the worst these parents do is forget their children, a situation the children meet with their wits with none of the terror of parental abandonment characteristic of previous children's stories. When Andy drives off with his mother, leaving Woody and Buzz behind, Woody asks in irritation, "Does he not even realize I am not there?" Then Woody, like the child protagonist in the *Home Alone* series, begins to make plans for getting back to Andy on his own. For children, perhaps, this downsizing of the adult evokes a laugh of liberation. For the adults, perhaps, this is a laugh of relief that acknowledges the possibility of building a complex relationship with children in which children are seen as changing and complex individuals and not unruly charges to be controlled.

However, the laughter is also premised upon an acceptance of the film's stance that there is no nonalienated self to be found and that the humiliations wreaked upon the worker since the eighties are not a cause for outrage. In laughing at Buzz's humiliations, we might be laughing at what Theodore Adorno and Max Horkheimer called schadenfreude, a "terrible laughter that overcomes fear by capitulating to the forces to be feared."[8] Miriam Hansen, reading Adorno and Horkheimer, clarifies in "Of Mice and Ducks" that humor can provide the glue that prevents the subject from recognizing himself or herself as the object of humiliation. In other words, Buzz's fantasies of an autonomous life take a beating in the film so that we can get accustomed to our instrumental use by capital in real life. Laughing at the adult worker as toy makes it possible to accommodate to the dismantling of the traditional labor movement since the Reagan-Bush years, as the cutbacks in social welfare programs, such as Medicaid, food stamps, school food programs, nutrition programs for women, energy assistance, and low-income housing subsidies; rising unemployment; and the shifting of production to the third world through free-trade agreements have acted together to compel labor to accept terms loaded against it.

Even at the most dramatic moment of transformation—when these toys come to life—they do not act autonomously but on behalf of an undefined, overarching system. They turn into socializing agents who discipline through surveillance rather than as love-denying parental or authority figures. Afraid that Sid will blow up Buzz, Woody hatches a plot with the toys in Sid's playroom to teach Sid a lesson. As Sid gets ready to blow up Buzz and grill Woody, the toys begin to speak. Warning Sid that they are everywhere, they command him to "play nice." As Sid shakes in fear, Woody announces: "We do not like being blown up. We—your toys. Take care of your toys. Because if you don't, we'll find out. We toys are everywhere. We will be watching you. So *play nice.*"

The toys become real to teach children not to violate the directions on the box, not out of respect for the uniqueness of each human but out of fear of a system that, like surveillance cameras, is everywhere, even in the playroom.

From Santa's Factory to the Company's Brand

The labor involved in toy production has been deeply mystified in children's narratives, as in capitalist ideology more generally. In the Santa Claus myth, it is literally banished to the end of the world. The North Pole crawling with elves, miniature nongendered adults indistinguishable from one another working under the directions of the kindly patriarch, Santa, is a barely disguised wishful image of the Fordist factory. The myth, like all long-living myths, has its internal contradictions. It recognizes such labor to be literally frozen in its isolation, even as it insists that the elves are quite content doing it. The elves are replaced in *Toy Story* by toys that introduce themselves by their brand names or countries of origin, that is, as already produced commodities. As the eyes and ears of an overarching system, they are merely its technical appendages.

Toy manufacturing and selling is a global business in which the third world provides cheap labor while the whole world literally is a market. In the year 2000, the National Labor Committee reported in *Toys of Misery*, $29.4 billion was spent on buying toys in the United States, with $837 million spent on advertising; of toys in the U.S. market, 80 percent are imported, with 71 percent imported from China. By 1995, Eyal Press reported in "Barbie's Betrayal," China's toy imports had swelled to $5.4 billion as compared with $237 million only ten years earlier. Subsequently, the number of U.S. workers employed in toy manufacturing, Press further reported, fell from 56,000 in 1973 to 27,000 in 2000. The toy industry has followed the logic of capital accumulation by seeking to diminish labor costs through shifting production to the third world, a task made easier by trade agreements like the North American Free Trade Agreement (NAFTA) and the General Agreement on Tariffs and Trade (GATT). Relocating production to the developing world is profitable because wages and benefits can be slashed, taxes avoided, health and safety standards disregarded, and workers fired for organizing, as national governments cooperate with U.S.-backed trade agreements.

The toy industry, driven by the major retailers like Wal-Mart, Toys R Us, and Target, and manufacturers like Mattel and Hasbro, is represented by the Toy Manufacturers Association, which has actively lobbied in favor of the trade agreements and against revoking China's most-favored-nation status so as to continue to sublet work to Chinese labor. The working conditions in these Chinese factories, according to the National Labor Committee and Press, are abysmal, with workers paid seventeen cents a day forced to work for sixteen hours a day in 104-degree temperatures handling toxic glues, paints, and solvents in repetitive, backbreaking, and sometimes injurious work. The mobility of global capital, however, is such that if China were to implement its labor laws, these toy manufacturers would move to Bangladesh or Honduras.

These political and economic realities of the toy market are lost in the laughter over Buzz's starry-eyed daydreams of wanting to be real and not a toy. The refusal of the toys to even conceive of a life outside of being a toy is the capitalist dream of a compliant worker.

Replacing the elves with brand identities in toy production is capitalism's repression of human labor, to the extent that it now occurs as a commodity even in children's playrooms.

Beanie Babies: The Humanization of the Commodity and the Commodification of the Human

While the analogy between the mechanical toy and the proletariat was met with indignation until the early part of the twentieth century, it is now met with equanimity even in children's culture. It is against this background that we can see the logical growth of Beanie Babies, who come packaged as commodified labor. Beanie Babies are retired—discontinued—at the will of Ty Inc., with the "retirements" announced on the company's Web page. Children are called upon to take an active part in acquiring the Beanie Baby by keeping up with the latest information on the Web site, then searching for outlets that sell the newest additions and buying them before they are "retired." Children are sold to as budding entrepreneurs who acquire Beanie Babies as an investment for their future value in the collectibles market.

The marketing strategy of Beanie Babies attempts to beat the glut in the children's market by making children want the brand and by making shopping itself into a game. How to introduce children to brands as early as possible and to teach them brand "loyalty" is an important area in market research. Among the advantages of teaching children brand loyalty, according to Guber and Barry in *Marketing to and through Kids*, is that it promises an extended period of buying as it also prepares future consumers. Early twentieth-century narratives like *The Velveteen Rabbit* tried to instill in children the importance of lasting human relationships by encouraging loyalty toward a particular toy. Beanie Babies, in contrast, attempt to teach loyalty to a corporate symbol, a brand. As consumers, children are repeatedly told to be wary of imitations, to recognize the "authentic" Beanie Baby by the tag around its neck. For my daughter's sixth birthday, I bought cheap imitations of Beanies to give as return gifts at the end of the birthday party. Children were quick to point out that these were imitations because they did not have the Ty logo around the neck. "Well, they are all still made in China," I replied. Of course, that fact would have to be pointed out again and again to make a dent in the myth that it is the company or capital that is the creative force.

Teaching brand loyalty is an attempt to overcome a contradiction inherent to capitalism. Competing over smaller and smaller niche markets, corporations constantly undermine loyalty to other brands by introducing products that are look-alikes of successful ones. The child consumer is encouraged to acquire the look-alike, to move on to the next fad, and then corporations complain of the fickle, whimsical consumer. The children's market is, as any children's-marketing textbook will testify, highly unpredictable, with a large number of fads that simply fail to generate a profit. The deliberate "retirement" of Beanie Babies is a marketing response precisely to this saturated toy market in which fad toys have an increasingly short life. A loyal consumer is an oxymoron, a capitalist's pipe dream on which millions are spent on advertising and research.

The toys in *Toy Story* mouth this megalomaniac vision of taming children's imaginations when they teach Sid the frightening lesson about following the directions on the box. For Sid is the fickle consumer. He, unlike Andy, breaks and recombines toys rather than mouth the pre-scripted narratives they come with. It is also no surprise that Sid's imagination is presented as nothing but violent. The other side of the freedom of the market for children is a removal of any protections for them; children confront the market on their own. In the capitalist imaginary, they can quite easily turn from desirable consumers into violent predators.

The marketing of Beanie Babies is an organized effort at redefining play as the consumption of market-produced commodities. To play with Beanie Babies is to enter a competitive game with other consumers against a marketing corporation that can arbitrarily withdraw any Beanie Baby from the market. Playing does not begin after a toy has been acquired. Rather, it ends with the acquisition of a toy and its addition to the collection. Play may resume at a later date when the child/adult reenters the market to sell the Beanie Babies at a higher price. Beanie Babies sprouted an industry, not directly sponsored by Ty Inc., that nevertheless aided its marketing. *The Beanie Baby Handbook*, a how-to book on Beanie Baby collection written for children by Les and Sue Fox, for example, calculates the possible price of different Beanies in the year 2007 and makes recommendations on which Beanies would fetch the highest price. These figures are based on mathematical calculations of the number of Beanies produced by relying on collector and dealer surveys and Ty Inc.'s gross sales. However, as the authors point out, all the estimated production figures may be wrong, because Ty Inc. does not divulge the quantities of Beanie Babies produced.

Further, there is no way of knowing how many Beanie Babies exist in good enough condition to compete in the future collectibles market.

Children are actively encouraged to buy Beanie Babies with an eye on the collectibles market—a market in children's objects that their own generation will nostalgically consume. In an article advising parents and kids on collecting "kids' junk," Janet Bodnar cautions against the vagaries of the market, suggesting that collecting children's toys is a gamble, given that "it's anyone's guess which comics or cards or toys will be popular—and how many of them will be around—20 years from now when today's kids try to recapture their childhood." To reconcile playing with collecting for the market, Bodnar has the following suggestion: "Buy duplicates—one to play with and one to keep in its box. The container can easily double an item's value."[9] Certainly, this is another ploy to make children buy more, but it also indicates the commodification of childhood. In other words, children are called upon to look at their childhood as a commodity, something outside them, something they have no particular rights over just because they are children. For this generation of children, childhood is already a museum object.

The Webs of Commodity Culture and Childhood's End

As the imaginative narratives of children's mass culture become indistinguishable from the marketing of commodities, and as children's movies become feature-length commercials, capitalism does indeed seem to tighten its web around children, drawing them into the market as consumers. *Toy Story*, for instance, could very well be one long toy commercial. Each of the toys in the film was available in the market in a variety of versions, as soft or plastic toys and also as CD-ROM games. While this is the first feature-length film in 3-D computer graphics, the technology has long been prevalent in toy commercials as a means to invest toys with personality and imaginative narratives. Called "character marketing," this strategy involves ascribing characters and narratives not only to toys but also to cereals, toothbrushes, and so on. This was a marketing ploy directed toward teaching brand loyalty by distinguishing similar toys from one another. Ascribing character to toys also invoked emotion rather than function, encouraging the child to buy more than one toy because of the different narratives surrounding it. The different roles Barbie dolls come with, such as the teacher Barbie, the nurse Barbie, Barbie on a date, and so on, were pioneers of this technique.

Toy Story's innovativeness lies in the precision with which the film translates adult genres into the marketing of children's toys, thus speaking to both the adults and the children in the audience. The romance between Little Bo Peep and Woody is set up along the conventions of a romantic comedy, while the toy soldiers parody the military action film. When the toy soldiers leave the playroom to report on the presents Andy gets on his birthday, they carry equipment such as a walkie-talkie, walk through plants and other household objects as if traversing a jungle, and subscribe to a militaristic code of ethics, including carrying an injured soldier. The marketing of Beanie Babies similarly invests toys with personality.

The inseparability of children's toys from ready-made narratives has led critics like Stephen Kline in *Out of the Garden* to conclude that children's play itself has become unimaginative, mechanical, and repetitive. There is little actual evidence to suggest this. These late twentieth-century narratives for children, just like their counterparts a century ago, tell us how childhood is imagined, not how it is lived. That the dominant capitalist imaginary now ridicules the possibility of a nonalienated life and constructs play as the buying and selling of commodities does not mean that play has indeed turned into consumption. Children still get attached to certain toys and keep them in spite of newer ones on the market; they change the meanings invested in these toys by marketing strategies; and they continue to play and invent games not yet commodified. *Toy Story*'s form too appeals to children. It presents a colorful, action-packed world in which the toys come to life in a three-dimensional space in a tone that is lighthearted.

However, what these new children's narratives tell us is that childhood is being redefined by capital here and now, before our eyes. For example, childhood is no longer imagined as a state separate from adulthood or as one embodied by children. In this conception, children have already become miniature adults, trying to generate profit through investments made over time. "It's our own personal 'theory of scarcity,'" write Les and Sue Fox in their how-to book on investing in Beanies, "that at least 90% of almost everything gets lost, stolen or destroyed within ten years. . . . Fires, floods, accidents, and life itself will simply take its toll. Whoever is lucky (and smart) enough to hang on to some top grade Beanie Babies for the long haul will be the future supplier of tomorrow's collectors."[10] That supplier in this imaginative reconstruction is sitting in the playroom, not playing but stashing away for the future. The question is, How does she or he escape the fires, floods, and life itself? Possibly by living in some isolated playroom, frozen in isolation, spending a lifetime calculating profit. Even now in some children's fiction, this description fits an old scrooge living by himself in a tower and counting his money.

Children, these narratives insist, have outgrown tales of nursery magic and playrooms sullied by money. The growing up of children, viewed with such alarm when it comes to children's knowledge of sex, arouses only a shrug or even a laugh when it comes to children's entry into the market as consumers. Meanwhile, capitalism continues to pull children into the market as consumers or labor (depending upon their class) and to redefine children as consumers and play as an engagement with the market either as entrepreneur or consumer.

The other side of this equation is that social protections granted to children are being systematically eroded. Cuts in health, education, housing, and legal protections granted to children under the juvenile-delinquent laws have been a consistent policy since the eighties. Under the current Bush regime, the Children's Defense Fund has found, the number of black children who live in extreme poverty—defined as a family of three living on $7,060 or less annually—has increased to one million, the highest level since 1980.[11] The inability of the middle- and working-class family to come between its children and the market is premised upon the following developments: (1) the end of households supported by the single income of the husband/father and a stay-at-home mother; (2) new technologies, such as faxes and emails and the reorganization of work, that make the home once again the sphere of work; and (3) the women's movement, which has challenged traditional gender roles.

The family is being called upon to stand as a fortress against capital, to take care of the sick, the elderly, and children precisely at the moment when capital, aided by new technologies, is breaking down its walls. Perhaps our political strategy should be to continue to demystify the public/private divide on which the family is based and call for socializing the care and nurture that families are called upon to provide.

The laughter at the passing away of old-fashioned tales of childhood could be an expression of relief at the end of the oppressive features of childhood and its imposed isolation from the world under authoritarian adult figures, if only it did not represent such compliance with the world as it exists. When children grow up in capitalism, they, like adults, are reduced to their market value.

5 The Children Who Need No Parents

"I've only one more question," he said. "What shall we do about our children?"
"Enjoy them while you may," answered Rashaverak gently. "They will not be yours for long."
It was advice that might have been given to any parent in any age: but now it contained a threat and terror it had never held before.
—Arthur C. Clarke, *Childhood's End*

Powerful science fiction, like good theory, defamiliarizes our present moment and makes us look at it as an unstable contingent condition from which a break with the past is possible. Challenging us to think of what the future might be if certain tendencies in the present are taken to their extreme although logical conclusion, science fiction makes us confront the present as a contested space for action.

In Arthur C. Clarke's 1953 novel *Childhood's End,* the parents faced a terror and threat of separation from their children unprecedented in human history because their children were poised to evolve into a species other than that of the parents, one so radically different that the parents could not even call it human. Consequently, there was no possibility of either a reunion or a reconciliatory understanding between these parents and children. Here Arthur C. Clarke contemplated the end of humanity and the birth of a new species that transcended the human—a transformation that is a tragic loss for the parents and a bold new adventure for the young, retelling once again modernity's persistent narrative of the new replacing the old, a narrative that is only further radicalized in postmodernity.

What was so new, almost "posthuman," about children that Clarke foresaw in 1953? First, Clarke's children ceased to exist as individual beings, becoming instead cells in a larger single entity he called the Overmind, a power that enveloped the entire universe. While Clarke's Overmind evoked religious belief, contemporary science fiction is equally apt to see in its place an all-pervasive, homogenizing consumer culture or a cybernetic technological factory that has killed the individual, transforming her or him into a zombified consumer or a cybernetic worker.

Jean Baudrillard, who has been at the forefront in announcing the victory of consumer culture and technology over human agency, claimed in "For a Critique of the Political Economy of the Sign" that affluent societies in the West were now primarily concerned with turning people into consumers. This was done systematically by subjecting people to an overarching code or system of signs that reference each other through advertising, fashion, marketing, and so on, producing a totalitarian system that runs by itself. Rather than see technology as the product of human society and as reflecting the economic, social, and political relations of that society, Baudrillard ascribes a logic and perfection to technology that is independent of human intervention, so much so that, as shown in *The Matrix* (1999), a film inspired by his writing, "society as a whole takes on the appearance of a factory" to which we are all subjected as consumers.[1]

Rob Latham, analyzing recent science-fiction texts, takes on an approach that, in contrast to Baudrillard's, is dialectical and locates cultural changes in the historical material transformation from a Fordist to a post-Fordist economy. Commenting on the preponderance of teenagers and even children as vampires and cyborgs in recent sci-fi, Latham incisively argues in *Consuming Youth* that these figures are metaphorical representations of the expansion of consumer culture, at the heart of which is a contest over the meaning of youth. Aptly named, his study focuses on the three ways in which consumer culture has shifted the social position of young people in the transition from a Fordist to a post-Fordist socioeconomic system. These are the widespread transformation of young people into consumers, the commodification of youth, and the fetishization of youth. The teenage vampires and cyborgs that inhabit this genre represent, according to Latham, the dialectical impulses of consumer culture: While it grants the young a certain autonomy by recognizing them as consumers, it in turn consumes youth by turning it into a commodity.

It can be added as a corrective to Latham's emphasis on consumer culture that capitalism also consumes the young by withdrawing social protections from them and consequently turning them into labor, subjecting children to the same exploitation as adults—a fact obvious in the characterization of poor black and Hispanic young people as "predators" and as existing everywhere in the third world, which continues to be the site of production that supports the consumer economy of the affluent nations, particularly the United States.

The second element that distinguishes Clarke's children from any known in human history is their innate ability to take care of themselves, making their parents entirely redundant. These children who can raise themselves and other children finally end the vulnerability of the human infant, which is biologically still more helpless than that of several other species. The baby who is still in the crib in Clarke's story, Jennifer Anne Greggson—the narrator refers to her by her full name, while the parents call her Poppet, as they had previously called her brother—can take care of all its needs. Her eyes remain forever closed in that defiant gesture of the young when they wish adults would disappear. As Clarke describes her: "To all outward appearances, she was still a baby, but around her now was a sense of latent power so terrifying that Jean [her mother] could no longer bear to enter the nursery."[2] Jennifer Anne can move the furniture, have her rattle shake by itself, make the food disappear from the refrigerator, and make the paint of the wall glow brighter. Not only can she survive, but she can also change her physical environment to suit her tastes.

Enter Matilda, the young heroine of the 1996 film of the same name. She too has magic powers, which she has acquired through her own concentrated efforts to raise herself in the face of her neglectful, self-centered, and imbecilic parents. By the age of six, Matilda can pour cereal and milk in her bowl without lifting a finger, rearrange the furniture in her classroom, make a videotape fly out of the car of two FBI agents right into her hands, and make their car roll down the road. In one sequence, she goes late one evening to the home of her tyrannical school principal, Miss Trunchbull, to teach her a lesson. She makes all the clocks turn, striking midnight. Trunchbull's portrait flies off from its place above the fireplace and into the fire, where we have the pleasure of seeing it slowly burn up. The lights go off and on, the sofa moves, and Trunchbull goes out of the house screaming. These could have been scenes from the horror-film genre of the seventies that included *The Exorcist* (1973) and *The Omen* (1976), except that *Matilda* is a film made for children, and these sequences not only parody the child of the horror film but also celebrate the self-reliant child.

Surely, some social transformation has come to pass that themes until recently the preserve of the sci-fi and horror genres—genres at the forefront of playing out social anxieties by displaying them in their extremes—should now have entered the family or children's film. William Paul has drawn attention in *Laughing Screaming* to the noticeable shift in children's role in the horror film, beginning with *The Bad Seed* (1956). Paul shows that following the Second World War, the child began to be represented as the monster rather than the victim in the horror film, a trend that reached its culmination in the seventies and the eighties, with *The Exorcist, The Omen*, and *Rosemary's Baby*. These films, according to Paul, show the dark side of the cult of domesticity in the postwar years.

The baby boom in the midst of economic prosperity, greater disposable income, and growth in consumer culture had made it possible to give children greater attention and more material comforts than ever before. This was reflected in the shifting approach to child care, which moved from the earlier strict schedules imposed upon the child to the child-centered practices advocated by Dr. Benjamin Spock and others. From children having to accommodate to adult's lives, it now seemed that adults had to mold their lives to adapt to their children's. By the seventies and the eighties, even the one or two children within the nuclear family were proving to be too much for it. Moreover, with the spread of children's consumer culture, it seemed that children were becoming adultlike and that parents were losing control over not only their children but also the ability to define, as Paul writes, the culture these children lived in. These repressed anxieties and hostilities that underlay the image of the happy fifties family came out in the horror genre's display of the nuclear family as the site of horror.

Also eclipsed by the image of the happy fifties family, Ilene Philipson explains in "Heterosexual Antagonisms and the Politics of Mothering," was the loneliness and unhappiness of middle-class women in the solitary confinement of the home. Until then the most educated generation of middle-class women, many of whom, unlike their mothers, had held jobs, they were asked to give it all up to marry and have children. Children were supposed to fulfill the emotional and social needs of adult women and were therefore seen and experienced as being both more valuable and more threatening in their neediness. Paul indicates that the child horror-film genre is also concerned with restoring patriarchal authority. It does so by showing the mothers to be singularly incapable of controlling their children, who in turn manipulate them. In other words, the evil child is a creation of the mother.

The Transition from Horror to Child's Play

To understand the social implications of the arrival in the children's film of the horror film's dark look at the family, let us begin by seeing how that look is carried over into these films, using *Matilda* as an example. The film revolves around the struggles of Matilda, an exceptionally bright girl who is ignored and unloved by her self-absorbed parents. Her father, Harry Wormwood, played by Danny Devito, calls her a "mistake." A used-car salesman, he is extremely proud of the profits he makes by swindling customers. His wife is Zinnia Wormwood (played by Rhea Perlman), whose main interest in life is playing bingo. Both of them are obsessed with their appearance and spend considerable time preening themselves—he with his hair oil and clothes (according to him, the customers buy him and not his cars), and she with her makeup and hair.

Matilda widens the horizons of her life beyond the narrowness of her parents' lives by learning to read on her own. At the age of four, she takes herself to the public library and begins devouring books on every subject, particularly what the narrator calls the "great" literary works, such as *Moby Dick* and Dickens's novels. Finally, when she is six, her father agrees to send her to school. The headmistress, Miss Trunchbull, is represented as a child-hating Nazi type, antifeminine, lesbian caricature. Her antithesis is Miss Honey, a bland paragon of virtue—white, thin, and very sweet. Miss Trunchbull is also Miss Honey's aunt and the cause of her unhappiness. She had killed Miss Honey's father and now lives in Miss Honey's large house, while Miss Honey lives poorly in a little cottage. By the end of the film, Matilda manages to wrest Miss Honey's house out of Trunchbull's clutches and frees herself from her parents, arranging her adoption by Miss Honey.

Matilda and Miss Honey then live happily ever after in Miss Honey's large house: Matilda can now begin being a child again, while Miss Honey has recovered her lost childhood. Not quite mother and child, the two live like girls, except one is years older. They rearrange the heavy furniture, clearing space for play, and picnic in girlish outfits. Moreover, since Miss Honey now is the new principal, children never want to leave school, and we have here the return of the perpetual childhood celebrated by the romantics a century and half earlier—

except that this state includes not only children who never grow up but also adults like Miss Honey. Most important of all, this Edenic garden is built by a clever-witted child who reclaims her childhood from bungling and incapable adults.

The Comedy of Adult Failure

The adult who is unable to control the child (most often the mother) evokes anger in the horror film—the child would not be such a monster if the mother would discipline it. Yet such adults are a source of great mirth in *Matilda*. The film, based on Roald Dahl's book, builds on his colorful caricatures of adults, mocking their efforts to rule children by ridiculing both the adults and the view that children should be dominated. To achieve this, Dahl has to first undo a premise that underlies the institution of childhood: that adults are more powerful than children, who in turn need their protection. Dahl denaturalizes this fundamental reality, caricaturing adult neglect of children as a subject of ridicule, not terror. In place of the mother in the horror film who loves her child "too" much to destroy the evil that faces her, or the adults who are so riveted by the innocent looks of the evil child that they cannot bring themselves to kill it, Dahl's inept adults are simply too preoccupied by their petty concerns to be bothered by the child.

Matilda's mother is caricatured as self-centered and petty but is not an ogre who threatens the child's very survival. Preoccupied with her gossip and makeup, she does not even notice the brilliance of her daughter. For instance, she lifts the baby Matilda out of her high chair to put her right into the kitchen sink to wash her like a dirty dish. While the mother mutters, "Babies," the camera moves on to reveal that Matilda, who has not yet started to walk, has spelt her name with spinach. Another day, Matilda comes home from school to find her mother sitting on the living-room couch, hair up in curlers and a contraption on her feet that holds her toes apart while she waits for the nail polish to dry. Upon seeing Matilda, the mother asks, without really expecting an answer, "How was school?" Matilda excitedly begins to talk, while her mother continues an animated phone conversation about abortion and men. The exaggerated makeup and clothes, silver curlers in the hair, feet up, toenails polished bright pink, all add up to a mother more concerned about her image than about the care of her child.

There is another striking sequence that reveals the vacuousness of the mother. One night, Matilda is crawling back to her room after having played a prank on her father. She has just replaced his hair oil with bleach. Suddenly her mother sits up and looks right at her. After an instant, we realize that she is wearing a sleep mask and is therefore not looking at Matilda. Her eyes are always so made up that it takes a second to see the difference. Again, this scene that could have evoked horror brings up laughter, because the child has tricked her foolish parents one more time.

The school principal, Miss Trunchbull, has the juiciest lines that indicate the preposterousness of adult authority over children. Her motto is "Use the rod and beat the child." She describes children as "useless," "Lilliputians," "insects," and so on. "A perfect school," according to her, "is one in which there are no children." Instead of talking to children, she hisses at them. One of her favorite activities is to throw children, something she considers good practice for her javelin throws, at which she is an Olympic champion. When alone in her own room, she throws darts at pictures of children. Trunchbull has a pronounced disgust for any evidence of cuteness on the part of children. When Amanda, a little girl, turns up with pigtails, Trunchbull asks her, "Do I allow pigs in my school, Amanda?" When Amanda replies that her mother thinks "they're sweet," Trunchbull responds, "Your mommy is a twit." She then proceeds to spin Amanda by her pigtails before throwing her over the school fence.

The caricature is highlighted by the costumes and the theatricality of Trunchbull's movements. Trunchbull wears military uniforms, big belts, and knee socks with heavy boots. Coupled with the hair pulled tightly back, a mustache, and her obsession with food and exercise, she is the prototype of the unfeminine. After killing Miss Honey's father, she takes charge of his chocolate box, refusing to share any candy with Miss Honey, who was then only a child. When it comes to chocolate cake, she cannot have enough of it, wiping it off the corners of her mouth as she gobbles it up greedily. The rest of the time she spends practicing her favorite sports, all of which involve hitting targets and throwing things. This fully grown adult woman is actually an overgrown bully who has not given up the oral fixations of childhood.

Matilda is filled with exaggerated adult-versus-child confrontations that reveal the ingenuity of the child and the idiocy of the adult. Matilda teaches her father a lesson for putting her down for her intelligence by hitting at his vanity when she replaces his hair oil with bleach and he ends up bleaching his dark hair. He then insists on going to work with a hat on, which Matilda manages to get glued to his head. It is Matilda who realizes that her father is under investigation by the FBI for stolen car parts, while her mother continues to entertain the agents, thinking they are selling boats.

Matilda's strongest victories are against Trunchbull. In one sequence, Trunchbull sets up an elaborate punishment for Bruce, a boy in the school who has stolen and eaten the chocolate cake made specifically for her. She asks Bruce to come up before the whole assembly. Seating him on a chair behind a large table on which lies a covered plate, she asks him to confess to eating the cake. When he refuses, she lifts the lid of the plate, revealing a luscious piece of chocolate cake. There is an extreme close-up on her hand as she lifts a large knife. Expecting the worst, the captive audience of children gasps in horror. Instead, Trunchbull simply asks Bruce to eat the cake. Bruce begins to eat it with trepidation (it may be poisoned) but realizes it is only a regular chocolate cake and finishes it with relish.

It is then that the punishment really begins. Trunchbull calls in the cook, who brings in an enormous cake, and Trunchbull commands Bruce to finish all of it. The cook is another caricature—an extremely thin and shriveled woman, it is as if all her juices had been soaked up in her cooking. As she leaves, wiping her nose on her sleeve, she says to the children, "See you at lunch." Bruce proceeds to eat the large cake but cannot go on and is almost ready to give up when Matilda stands up and cheers him on. To the cheers of the entire assembly, Bruce licks the plate clean, burps loudly, and holds up the empty plate like a trophy to the cheering crowd. Trunchbull is defeated and the children victorious.

Matilda finally wrests from Trunchbull both the school and Miss Honey's house. Not only does she terrify Trunchbull in the privacy of her home, but also she has other nasty surprises waiting for Trunchbull in school the next day, so that the other children too get to enjoy the fall of this big bully. Trunchbull arrives in Matilda's class hoping to scare the children into revealing who was responsible for the events of the previous night. Instead, she finds a repeat of last night's performance. As she watches in horror, the blinds begin to open and shut by themselves, creating a pattern of light and shade on the walls. A piece of chalk flies through the air and begins to write by itself. As if possessed by the spirit of Miss Honey's dead father, it writes:

Agatha
This is Magnus. Give my little Bumble Bee her house and her
money. Then get out of town. If you don't I will get you. I will
get you like you got me. That is a promise.

Trunchbull makes a last-ditch attempt to assert her superior physical
power. She picks up a boy and throws him out the window. Matilda
uses her powers to bring him gliding back. He crashes into Trunchbull,
throwing her on a large globe, which Matilda spins around, ending
the last semblance of Trunchbull's power and control. Trunchbull walks
out of the school with children throwing their lunches and toilet paper at her and is never heard from again.

Outing the Power between
Adults and Children

The horror film, too, plays on the anomaly of the
far greater physical power of the adult being overtaken by the child.
We see children killing adults (*The Omen* and *The Exorcist*) and even
cannibalizing them (*The Night of the Living Dead*, 1968). However,
in the horror film the issue of power between children and adults is
elided by displacing it onto either an individual child's pathology or
some unnatural intervention. Paul astutely observes in *Laughing
Screaming* that fantasy such as satanic possession or genetic manipu-
lation is used in these films to express the psychological experience
of the isolation and demanding nature of raising children within the
privatized family, such that children are perceived as in control of their
parents' lives. By casting the demanding child as satanic, these films
open up the space to give full play to these very real resentments against
children, which would otherwise be taboo.

Matilda outs this adult secret, making what was once a tale of horror into one of delightful celebration. It exposes the power between
adults and children from the point of view of the child and caricatures it, both through its elaborate mise-en-scènes and dialogue. Not
only does the camera shoot Trunchbull from the children's perspective, making her a giant, but also she is given lines that unambigu-
ously display her boorishness: "I am big and you are small; I am smart
and you are dumb; I am right and you are wrong; and there is nothing you can do about it." Harry Wormwood repeats this litany when
he insists that Matilda obey him. Leaning over and thrusting his face

into hers, he says: "I am big and you are small; I am right and you are wrong." The words that ring like a mantra only reveal the stupidity of the claim, since they are repeated by adults who are vain, dimwitted, shallow, and crass compared to the child to whom they utter them. This direct confrontation with the issue of power as it appears from the perspective of the child takes the scare out of the horror film and makes it a laughable matter.

The child of the horror genre is demystified at another level as well. A presumption that underlies the evil-child-possessed-by-Satan trope is that ultimately the child is an empty vessel, only in this case it is possessed by evil rather than good. Matilda, however, is no blank slate. Rather, she has acquired magical powers through her own will and effort, motivated by the desire to take charge of her own life. Strikingly, she begins to acquire these powers when she realizes in response to her father's taunts that children are also persons.

Contrary to being possessed, Matilda owns herself. Quite appropriately, she chooses her own guardian rather than be tossed around in custody battles. Toward the end of the film, when her parents come looking for her as they are escaping to Guam on a permanent vacation, she puts her adoption papers in front of her mother and asks her to allow Miss Honey to adopt her. "I have had these adoption papers ever since I could use the Xerox machine," she tells her mother, who, not a mean woman, signs the papers. Here she echoes what has long been a demand of children's rights activists like John Holt that choosing their guardians should be one of the basic rights of children.[3]

The Deconstruction of Childhood and the Transition to Late Capitalism

The excessive surveillance of the child by the middle-class, usually white, isolated stay-at-home mother of the fifties has by the nineties conclusively given way to the phenomenon of "home-alone" kids. Taken from the title of a popular film series, *Home Alone,* the phrase captures a social trend, indicating how a popular media reference becomes part of common parlance and is both a reflection of and construction of a social reality. Home-alone kids are basically children who are increasingly responsible for raising themselves. Also called "latchkey children" in Britain, they are youngsters who come home after school to a house without a parent, fix their own lunches, and organize their time without direct adult supervision. This is an outcome of the increased inability of middle- and working-class families to provide full-time care to children in the home, and of new technologies that have indeed made it possible for children to take care of themselves.

In each of the *Home Alone* films, the plot revolves around a child who is forgotten by his parents and manages in the world by his wits. In *Home Alone* (1990), the child protagonist, Kevin, a boy of six or seven, is left alone at home by his parents, who leave for their Christmas vacation without him. He manages to outwit the two bumbling thieves who try to break into his large suburban house. In *Home Alone 2* (1992), Kevin gets lost at the airport and ends up in New York instead of Florida, where his family is headed for a vacation. This time he manages by his wits in the big city, outwitting the same two thieves, who have escaped from jail. *In Home Alone 3* (1997), Kevin is left alone sick at home by his mother, who has to attend to an important appointment at work. He manages to outwit an international set of criminals who are after a nuclear device that has been mistakenly placed in his toy car.

While both the home and the city are presented as sites of danger, the child is shown to be completely capable of dealing with them and of emerging victorious—an imaginary resolution that adults and children need to soothe their anxieties about coping with an economy incapable of providing full-time adult care to children, even for the middle class. By the end of the twentieth century, middle-class children, like their working-class counterparts, are typically growing up either in families where both parents work in wage-paying jobs or in single-parent families; in the year 2000, as Hochschild points out in *The Commercialization of Intimate Life*, two-thirds of women with children under the age of six were in the labor force.

Moreover, capitalist expansion and new technologies have expanded the working day, creating flexible work schedules that move well into the nights and weekends, so that children might well be home alone in the presence of a parent who is working. These flexible schedules are not primarily motivated by the desire to integrate children into adult life or to meet the needs of taking care of children. Rather, they are necessitated by the demands of a global economy that knows no rest. Harriet Presser, studying the changes in the nature of work in the U.S. economy, finds that only one-third of U.S. workers in 1991 were employed in full-time jobs, that is, in a nine-to-five, Mondaythrough-Friday workweek.[4] Consequently, middle-class children are increasingly called upon to take care of themselves and their younger siblings.

This task is made possible by new technologies such as microwaves, which enable children to cook for themselves, and television and the Internet, which provide insights into the world that an adult caregiver might have provided. Add to this frozen lunches and dinners packaged specifically for children, and you have children who are far more self-sufficient than in any earlier generation. A generation born amidst far greater technological intervention than ever before—beginning right from conception (through IVF, sperm banks, ultrasounds) through the infant years (with teddy bears that imitate sounds of the womb, flashcards and boom boxes that prepare children to use a keyboard before they learn to write) to the preteen years—it seems that our children, like Clarke's children fifty years ago, stand poised to change the very meaning of what it is to be human.[5]

Called by some a generation of cyborgs, today's children are now seen to have abilities that make them grow up faster than before. Writing on children's play with video games, Marsha Kinder contends that these interactive games empower children, giving them a sense of fluid identity. While this socializes them into the culture of consumption (you can invent your identity through what you buy), it also accelerates perceptual-cognitive development in striking new ways, developing skills in processing visual information from multiple perspectives and iconic-spatial representation once restricted to elite technical occupations, such as pilot and engineer.[6]

Kinder's insight that children today are handling technology once the preserve of adults is strikingly similar to Marx's observation more than a century earlier that the machine had so simplified and fragmented labor that it enabled the transformation of children into instruments for capital. The ten-hour working day won for children in Massachusetts in the second half of the eighteenth century, Marx bitterly pointed out, was in England until the seventeenth century "the normal working day of able bodied artisans, robust labourers, athletic blacksmiths."[7] Cyborgization, the process of extending the human with human-made technological interventions, is certainly not new in human history. However, its pace has radically accelerated over the last two centuries, a phenomenon that underlies the anxiety that every new generation is unrecognizable to its parents. Marx did not view cyborgization with complete horror. In fact, for him the machine extended the productive capabilities of the human, making it possible to finally end scarcity, thus creating the material basis for the truly "rich human being," one who would be in "need of a totality of human life-activities—the man in whom his realization exists as an inner necessity, as need."[8]

It is capitalist relations that obstruct human self-realization by reducing the human to the dead-end goal of capitalist accumulation in fewer and fewer hands. The logic of private capital accumulation cannot accommodate the rational and socialized organization of our wealth and resources to meet human needs such as education, health, housing, and child care. Industrial capitalism, in partnership with the patriarchal ideology of the essential separation between men and women, left to women the task of providing care and nurturing. Children, pulled out of the factory and adult life, were seen to naturally belong to the home and the school. The home-alone child is a product of capital's pulling women into the market (aided by feminism) without socialized care for children. The cyborg human child, far more capable than its predecessors and with access to experiences and a world wider than ever before, stands trapped within the walls of domesticity, as alone as the individualist bourgeois adult.

The Politics of Class and the Deconstruction of Childhood

Films like *Matilda* and *Home Alone* assuage our anxiety about leaving children to fend for themselves by insisting that children are quite capable of looking after themselves. The shift from sci-fi or horror to the children's film indicates that what was perceived to be an extreme situation is now an accepted social reality. However, there is one feature of the sci-fi and horror film that is missing in these children's films: These children, for all their self-sufficiency, do not threaten to turn into another species altogether unrecognizable to their parents. On the contrary, Kevin is only too happy to revert to being a child when his parents return home—until the next sequel—and Matilda, the film's narrator tells us, chose her own "style," dressing herself up in pastel dresses and ribbons that evoke the girl children from the early twentieth century. Matilda is the image of the idealized child we know from classic children's literature, not the cyborg child evoked by sci-fi. By the end of the film, Matilda even demurely agrees to give up her magic powers, albeit only temporarily, for she does not need them anymore.

These narratives manage to retain the old image of the child in spite of having played out the new by retaining the notion that the bourgeois family is the ideal place to raise a child. *Home Alone* does so by painting Kevin's upper-middle-class professional parents as overworked and absent-minded but essentially caring parents. *Matilda*, in contrast, ridicules the parents. However, the launching pad of its attack on the parents is based on an elitist distaste for the upwardly mobile petty bourgeois. The Wormwoods, as their name signifies, are rotten, hollow people who do not fit into the upper-class neighborhood they live in. They have come into money recently through Harry Wormwood's dubious dealings in his used-car business. The narrator makes it clear that they are misfits in the "nice"—that is, upper-class suburban—neighborhood. Harry's and his wife's garish clothes, their brightly colored house filled with appliances, such as a used television set that Harry bought cheap, all signify their low taste.

The Wormwoods' home is a contrast to the huge Victorian home of Miss Honey. Instead of the portraits and clocks that hang on her walls, the trees and the bushes that surround the house, or the several rooms, including the attic and the kitchen, that create layers and secrecy around Miss Honey's house, the Wormwoods' house could be the set of a television show. Lacking any depth, the entire first floor can be seen in one shot. Zinnia Wormwood's kitchen is a storehouse of prepackaged frozen foods. The most she assembles in it is breakfast, bowls of colorful cereal served in equally colorful plastic bowls.

Worst of all, this family loves the set. They are the kind of low-culture, poor-taste family that dominates the conservative "end-of-childhood" discourse. At the head of this family is a father whose authority is a mockery of the patriarch. The only power he has is over the TV remote control. There is a central sequence in the film that establishes this. Earlier in the day, Matilda had managed to get her father's hat glued to his head. Her mother had just cut it off, but a band still circles the father's head, which now sports bleached hair. Furious, the father switches on the television and commands that everyone watch TV and eat their dinners. TV dinners are laid out on collapsible tables in front of every member of the family. The show they watch is called *Sticky*, a game show in which people covered in glue roll around in a glass cage, trying to get floating dollar bills to stick to their bodies.

Matilda sits with the family but instead of watching the show reads *Moby Dick* by the dim light of a lamp beside her. Her father gets up and asks her if she belongs to this family. He demands that she watch television like the rest of them, that she act "like a Wormwood." When she continues to read, he holds her head between his hands and forces her to watch the television show. It is a highly exaggerated scene in which the television light plays on the family's faces, showing them as something grotesque out of a television show themselves. Matilda stares in anger at the television set, which suddenly blows up. This is the first use of her extraordinary powers. Smashing the television set is a favorite remedy for those who call for a return to the old-fashioned family.

Identifying television as "low" culture, the film makes a case for the "great" books. Matilda's parents are shown as worthless because they do not read and have no respect for education; they have come into the upper middle class through quick moneymaking schemes rather than inherited wealth or long years of professional training. Television, according to Harry Wormwood, is the way to learn about everything. "It makes things easy, so why read books?" he asks. When Miss Honey visits Matilda's family, thinking that her parents must be responsible for inculcating in Matilda her love for reading, she is shocked to find that they would rather watch television than talk to her. Here, in another moment of Dahl's exaggerated comedy, Zinnia Wormwood responds with complete disdain to Miss Honey's assertion that Matilda will go to college. Comparing herself to Miss Honey, she says in simple rhyme: "I chose looks and you chose books; I have a nice house, a wonderful husband, and you work with snot-nosed children all day teaching them their ABCs."

"Don't sneer at educated people," replies Miss Honey righteously, her hand on her heart.

Of course, this downgrading of television, put there by a children's author, not by a television executive, is a good example of self-promotion. Matilda has to walk to the public library and read books rather than search the Internet to broaden her horizons. This emphasis on books is a call for the old hierarchy between adults and children. The printing press, Aries has pointed out in *Centuries of Childhood*, helped invent childhood, as it enabled the separation of the worlds of adults and children. As literacy replaced oral culture, it instituted a long period of apprenticeship for children, who had to learn to read in school and in the family. In *The Disappearance of Childhood*, Postman holds television's audio-visual culture responsible for breaking down this hierarchy. Television, according to Postman, blurs the boundaries between entertainment and news, making the world seem to be out of control and irrational. He suggests restoring childhood by adults' asserting authority and shutting the television set off.

Here we see once again that the growing up of the young, an extension of their power made possible by technology and to a limited extent by their status as consumers, is perceived as a threat not only to the hierarchy of children and adults but also ultimately to the status quo of society more generally. After all, if children separate from their parents, they stand to invent a new society in which the older norms of class, gender, race, and sexuality may no longer operate. Choosing to focus only on technology, the spread of consumer culture, or the relationship between children and adults to the exclusion of the overarching domination of capital and the specific ways in which the bourgeois home is under transformation leads to a reactionary call for the old-fashioned family with the old-fashioned child at its center.

Consequently, *Matilda*'s response to the new is to call for the old, even if it requires the conceit that a child, having acquired powers of self-sufficiency, will willingly give them up. At the end of the film, Matilda turns into a child and lives in a place from a past century: a large Victorian house filled with books, where there is no television or Internet or video games, and time is spent having tea parties and picnics. However, like *Home Alone*, *Matilda* does not reinstate the authority of the patriarch. In the former, both parents manage the home and children more or less as equals; in the latter, Matilda lives with Miss Honey, who is a grown-up girl herself. However, there is one element of the bourgeois family that is kept intact in both films: The family is presented as the site of private property outside of the market.

This is the dialectic of the entry of the self-sufficient child from the horror film into the children's movie under late capitalism. While such a child becomes a subject of celebration, testifying to the new autonomy granted children by new technologies and their recognition as consumers, it tames that threat by putting the child back into the private family. Returning the child home, however, both narratives recognize as a temporary solution: Matilda has only given up her powers for the moment, and Kevin is at home with his parents only until the next time they forget him.

6

The Burdens
of Time in
the Bourgeois
Playroom

*The mystical feeling which drives the philosopher
forward from abstract thinking to intuiting is
boredom—the longing for a content.*

—Karl Marx

Lewis Carroll's *Alice in Wonderland* opens by telling us: "Alice was beginning to get very tired of sitting by her sister on the bank, and of having nothing to do" (1). Chris Van Allsburg's *Jumanji*, written almost eight decades later, describes the game Jumanji as "a young people's jungle-adventure especially designed for the bored and the restless." Many a modern children's tale begins as a way to alleviate the heaviness of frozen time as it hangs over the isolated child in the bourgeois playroom. Boredom—the dread of having absolutely nothing to do, which is experienced both as a failure and disability—is a specific response to the commodification of experience under capitalism, an outcome of the absurd expectation generated by consumer culture that life should be an endless procession of opportunities to expand the self through the acquisition of things. A longing for content, it is a search for the sensuous nonalienated life, both for the philosopher lost in the abstract history of the idea and the consumer amidst the continuous parade of spectacles and events.[1] For Marx, nonalienated life begins when human development becomes a need and an end in itself; like children's play, the work of an artist or of revolution-making nonalienated labor begins with a sensuous engagement with the material world in an effort to change it.

The English word "boredom" has a history of not more than two centuries. First appearing in the middle of the eighteenth century, it was used as both a noun and a verb to connote a dismissive attitude toward a thing which bores.[2] Hyunsuk Seo, reading Siegfried Kracauer, Charles Baudelaire, and Walter Benjamin, suggests that these astute observers of early twentieth-century consumer culture saw boredom as a profoundly contradictory experience: It was experienced as a state of both malign distress and liberating estrangement.[3] To be bored and not to be agonized by it is at its best, Seo suggests, a political act or at the very least, as noted by Adam Phillips in *On Kissing*, a sign of psychological maturity. After all, as Phillips points out, it is a voluntary disengagement from the glittering world of commodities. Profound boredom, Kracauer suggests in this light, is the only "proper occupation, an event in which one is with oneself and in control of one's existence."[4]

However, boredom is designated a malady in capitalism because it amounts to wasting time. Capital transforms time into a commodity, that is, it has exchange value that can be measured in money. Time is the basic unit against which profits are calculated, and therefore the capitalist work ethic is a struggle against time, to make every minute yield ever more profits. Wasting time is also perceived as a *personal* failure because the bourgeois imagines that the individual precedes society, which is comprised of individuals who enter into contracts with others.

Capitalist expansion in the late twentieth century has consistently eroded the boundaries, including domestic space, that stand in the way of maximizing the use of time to generate profits through both production and consumption. Thanks to new technologies such as computers, faxes, and cell phones, even travel spaces—airports, train stations, and hotels—that had previously enforced a waiting period are now colonized as spaces of work and entertainment or consumption. Reinhard Kuhn, elaborating in *The Demon of Noontide* on the degrees of boredom, contrasts the inactivity of the mind enforced by external circumstances such as travel, which he calls the simpler boredoms, with anomie, the total loss of the will to live.

Clearly, boredom as a political withdrawal from consumer culture is a class privilege. It assumes the ability to buy and is therefore quite different from the boredom of a repetitive job that must be done to make a living. Third-world street children, for example, do not have the luxury to be bored by the offerings of fast-food chains. Nevertheless, the withdrawal of the consumer into boredom strikes at the core of capital, because the failure to buy nullifies the capital invested in creating the commodity, for it cannot be turned into profit. Capital cannot be accumulated if the consumer is simply too bored to buy or to make another trip to the mall, which is why we have the disciplines of capitalism, such as marketing, consumer behavior studies, advertising, and mall architecture, all centered on finding ways to make us shop one more time.

While capitalist ideology treats boredom as a sickness, asking how one can get bored when surrounded by five hundred television channels and entertainment at every turn, it is in fact the authentic experience of an alienated life, of both the worker and the consumer. As Baudelaire described the symptoms of boredom in his diary: "What I feel is an immense discouragement, an unbearable sense of isolation, a perpetual fear of some vague evil, a complete distrust of my powers, a total absence of desire, an impossibility of finding any sort of amusement."[5]

So profoundly disturbing is the experience of boredom in modernity that childhood, its antidote, is imagined free of it. Fearing the disenchantment of boredom, adults reinforce children's dismay at the experience of boredom, Adam Phillips notes, through relentless efforts to distract the child, as if the adults have decided that the child's life must be, or be seen to be, endlessly interesting.[6]

Children, imagined as the other of modernity, as neither consumers nor workers, waiting as it were to grow into this world, cannot help but experience adult emotions, including boredom. This is so because childhood, an invention of modernity, does not exist outside capitalism. To consider children as outside of capital is similar to the view that the third-world artisan produces work that is the opposite of mass-manufactured goods (that it is unique and handmade while the latter are mass-produced). This notion obfuscates the fact that the artisan is integrated into the global economy and that the value of his or her handmade product is based on that integration.

Boredom is, in fact, natural to the state of childhood, which Alfred Hitchcock so insightfully characterized as "life's great waiting room in which we while away the hours until our driver's license is issued."[7] Waiting rooms are among the most boring of places within the capitalist logic of maximizing the use of time; they impose aimless spending of time that has to be passed or killed until, for example, the awaited train arrives. While in Lewis Carroll's imagination the waiting served as a sanctuary from the inevitable onslaught of the market, in the marketer's lexicon of the late twentieth century it provides a captive audience for products. Carroll's Alice wove dreams out of her boredom that revealed to her the bizarreness underlying what was passed off as normal adult behavior. Here boredom was the necessary stage that moves the child, like Marx's philosopher, into intuiting the illogical nature of adult life that she will soon have to embark upon. From the standpoint of the market, however, boredom is an unnecessary annoyance that the child has to be distracted from by giving her several market choices. The cause of the problem is presented as its cure. Consequently, capital continues to inundate the child with an ever-changing spectrum of commodities, boring the playroom to the point of explosion.

Perhaps recognizing the wild fantasies that children weave in the hours spent alone in the playroom, Walter Benjamin characterized boredom as "the dream bird that hatches the egg of experience. A rustling in the leaves drives him away."[8] A state of extreme inertia, it is potentially the site from which a new subversive alternative might be found, turning the bored child into a potent threat. The threat many media reports have shocked the Western world with is the torture and killing of teenagers and children by other teenagers, sadistic not only in their violence but in their presentation as spectacle, as teenagers videotape themselves in these acts.[9] While this certainly is a cause for alarm and should wake us up, it would be wrong to conclude that the solution is an all-out war against the young in which they have to be returned to adult control under the family and the school.

Instead, we would benefit from an analysis of the causes that underlie the emotional experience of boredom. To admit that children could experience the same loss of curiosity, absence of desire, and lack of ambition as that described by Baudelaire is to admit to producing a generation that has lost the will to live and therefore to call for an end to a structure that wrought this. To understand boredom, we need to understand the culture industry that attempts to alleviate the malady with the very thing that causes it—excess, spectacle, and the expectation of constant novelty. It is for this reason that I analyze how Hollywood, itself a dream machine, shows us the fantasies that the "dream bird" brings to the bourgeois playroom. How does it represent a state that it has been so instrumental in creating?

The Specter of Boredom and the
Collapse of the Bourgeois Playroom

Jumanji (1995), based on the book of that title by Chris Van Allsburg, brings to the screen the fantasies unleashed out of boredom. What is striking about Van Allsburg's books is the predominance of the image to the telling of the story. In fact, one of his books, *The Mysteries of Harris Burdick*, relies almost completely on illustrations. The pictures evoke a strong sense of mystery, challenging the reader to read them imaginatively and to explore the nooks and crannies that exist in their three dimensionality. Unlike the illustrations that are the usual fare of children's books, these pictures evoke the visible, the material world, as deeply mysterious and unknown.

One of the recurrent themes in Van Allsburg's stories is that the perception of mystery or magic is highly elusive, private, and incompatible with the outside world. It is also the prerogative of the child. In his *Polar Express*, the child protagonist who had made an enchanted journey to the North Pole and received a bell from Santa can no longer hear the bell as an adult. However, unlike the imagined children of the romantics, filled by nature with curiosity and wonder, Van Allsburg's children have to learn these attributes, and his writings and drawings are meant to serve as aids to this end. Like Jack, from the film of the same name, and Matilda, Van Allsburg's children are born as grown ups who then have to reclaim their childhoods.

In the book *Jumanji*, a brother and sister, Peter and Judy, one afternoon find a board game called Jumanji. Their parents have left them alone for the evening, and once the children have thrown around all the toys they already own, they are bored and go out in the search of something new. They find the game abandoned in a park and at first have no high expectations for it, since it looks like so many other board games they already have. Disenchanted consumers, they are at first skeptical of the game's ability to interest them, particularly since it is also free. "I am sure," says Peter, "somebody left it here because it's so boring."

Once they start playing, however, the game unleashes all kinds of fantastic happenings in the house—mosquitoes, monkeys, lions, spiders, monsoons, a stampede, and a man with a gun. Once they have started playing, the children have to finish the game to reverse all that has happened. Peter and Judy succeed in finishing the game, and their parents return to find them unusually tired but with nothing out of place. The parents have no idea what has gone on. Like his other stories,

Van Allsburg ends this one with an open question. You, the reader, have to decide whose version of the story you are going to believe: the children's or the parents'. What you believe is an act of choice that calls upon you to take sides with either children's imagination or adult rationality.

The 1996 film begins with the same plot but departs in fundamental ways that both radicalize and tame the story. First, it completely erases boredom as the starting point of the children's adventure. It replaces Peter and Judy, who are typical bourgeois children, with Alan (played by Robin Williams), who is developed as a lonely boy deeply alienated from his wealthy and authoritarian father. The narrative economy of Hollywood filmmaking, where every shot has to count toward keeping the viewer engaged in the rush of images that tell a story, cannot allow time for aimless wandering, let alone create banal everyday time that oppresses the audience. Boring the audience would belie the basic premise of an industry that has served as an object lesson for consumer culture—promising constant novelty and excitement, and building the motivation to make the most out of one's time. The film uses every available cinematic technique and special effect, neatly tied into cause-and-effect relations, to heighten suspense and keep the narrative from ever slowing, let alone approaching the psychological state of boredom.

However, in depicting the fantasies unleashed by boredom, the film goes much further than the book. It moves the wild events out of the privacy of the home into the outside world and in so doing vividly expresses the sense of a world run amok. It shows a world that is out of control—adults act like children; children act like adults; people remember not just the past but also the future; people die before they are born; people do not play games but games play people; and children's fantasies and imaginations threaten not only to subvert the home but also to spill out into the streets.

While *Jumanji* is commonly accepted as a children's book—it is usually found in the children's section of the public library or of the local bookstore—there has been a difference of opinion about the appropriateness of the film as one for children. Many adults find it frightening, fearing, one suspects, the story's evocation of the powerlessness of the child's state and its eruption into daydreaming that threatens to explode the feelings of anger, hostility, sexuality, and violence trapped within the confines of a supposedly happy childhood. The film, with its playful use of conventions from the horror genre and special effects from sci-fi, presents the unleashing of these emotions as both exhilarating and alarming. The use of these genres, one often associated with the past and the other with the future, is particularly poised to bring out the turmoil of childhood as a state trapped in between the two.

The opening scene sets the date 1869 over a dark screen that fades to reveal two boys, possibly brothers, burying an old chest. The mise-en-scène evokes the horror-film genre, foregrounding the primitive and dangerous nature of what is to come. We hear the neighing of a horse and the howling of wind and wolves as the two boys stand in the dark woods lit by a solitary lamp in one of the boys' hands. The boys dig a hole and bury the chest. "What will happen if someone finds it?" asks the younger boy. "Then may God have mercy on his soul," replies the older.

The next shot is a sharp contrast. It is a bright sunlit day in a small town marked by white fences, trees, and grass as the camera follows a boy on his bicycle who is helped across the street by a policeman. On the screen appear the words "1969, Bradford, New Hampshire." The camera follows Alan Parrish, the ten-year-old son of the richest man in town. Mr. Parrish owns a shoe factory for which he is grooming his son and heir and claims a long ancestry of wealthy Parrishes.

Alan Parrish, for his part, is terribly lonely. Mocked by other boys for being a daddy's boy and a Parrish, he is also pushed away by his distant and authoritarian father. His mother is more or less a decorative piece who tries to intervene on Alan's part with the father, but both are keen to send Alan to a boarding school founded by the Parrishes. What stretches out before Alan is another long period of isolation, and he decides to run away from home. However, on a visit to the factory, he finds the game Jumanji buried in a construction site close by. The game draws Alan toward itself with its incessant drumbeat that is like both a primitive tribal beat and a beating heart. It is a sound that can be heard only by children, in particular those who are unhappy. Alan brings the game home. Once home, however, he forgets about it and sets about preparing to run away.

As he is leaving the house, Sarah Whittle, who is the bully's girlfriend but whom Alan also likes, knocks at his door. Both start playing the game, which is rendered with special effects common to video games that evoke the futuristic sci-fi-genre film. When Sarah first rolls the dice, the children hear strange animal screeches. Sarah asks Alan to put away the game but before he can do so the dice slip out of his hands. "The game thinks I rolled," declares Alan in fear, reminiscent of sci-fi films where games and objects acquire lives of their own. Alan's hands grow long and thin and so does his body until he is sucked into the game, never to be seen again. Sarah runs out of the house with bats chasing her down the street.

The story then takes up twenty-six years later in 1995. In a remarkable elliptical gesture, we see the change in time via a close-up of the large golden doorknobs inside the house, which have now rusted and the doors' wood decayed. The viewer, like Alan's unfinished childhood, is made to sit trapped inside the home until the door opens to let in Peter and Judy. Alan's house is bought by Peter and Judy's aunt, a young single woman who takes care of them after their parents' deaths. Peter and Judy are compulsively drawn to the game, which has lain all this time in the attic. The rest of the film dwells at length on all the extravagant things—one of them Alan Parrish—that are released from the game. To release themselves from the spell of the game and turn everything back to normal, Alan and Sarah must join Judy and Peter and finish a game they started twenty-six years earlier. All four of them manage to complete the game, and Alan is turned into a little boy again. Alan's father returns to find his ten-year-old son ready to make peace with him.

Time Travel and Shifting Identities

A basic theme in the film *Jumanji* is time travel—going back and forth in time between the past and the future. The film vividly materializes, in its narrative and in its emphasis on computer-generated spectacle, the idea of moving through time. Time can be undone the same way film can be rewound, fast-forwarded, and replayed. Tom Gunning has pointed out in "The World as Object Lesson" that early cinema, like the technologies of railways and the wireless, offered "virtual voyages" that collapsed the distinction between the tourist and the spectator. Anne Friedberg, among others, has continued the argument that new media technologies such as television, VCRs, multiplexes, computers, and virtual reality give the spectator "new freedoms" over the body—"the race-, gender-, age-, and class-bound body could be 'implanted' with a constructed (albeit ideological) virtual gaze." The spectator who can rewind, fast-forward, and freeze frames is "lost in and also in control of time." The media proliferating around us, Friedberg continues—"invading the everyday with images produced, repeated, returned to, simultaneously preserved and instantaneously obsolete—has produced a shifting, mobile, fluid subjectivity."[10]

This ability to transcend given identities imaginatively through time and space has significant consequences for childhood. Its implications are that childhood and adulthood are attributes that can be experienced at any time. This is, however, a result not simply of new technologies but also of the ways in which new technologies are integrated into capitalist relations. As I have reiterated throughout this book, the adult-child polarity is broken by the mass-scale transformation of children into consumers, thus granting them a public recognition denied them in earlier times as dependent upon adults. The process is parallel to the construction of women as consumers in the early part of the twentieth century, because of which women were recognized as somewhat autonomous of men, at least to the extent that they could exercise consumer choice.[11]

Further, consumer culture promises adults youth as an end in itself, thus producing a generation of adults that Ron Goulart diagnosed as suffering from a "Peter Pan complex," that is, adults who are unable to grow up or who grow up falsely.[12] Investing huge amounts of money, time, and effort in holding on to youthful bodies, the baby-boom generation has turned youth from an attribute of the young into, as Lawrence Grossberg writes, a state of mind that has to be held on to by cultural and physical effort.[13] Consequently, we have the phenomenon of what Joshua Meyerowitz describes as "the childlike adult and the adultlike child," in which children are becoming increasingly sophisticated and adults juvenilized.[14]

One of the manifestations of this permeability is the popular discourse of inner-child therapies, in which adults are called upon to nourish and restore the child within them, the child who may have suffered in abusive relationships with its guardians. As Marilyn Ivy points out in her insightful essay on such therapies, they call for a series of splits within the subject. One takes up a variety of positions within oneself —victim and comforter, child and adult, patient and therapist. It is, Ivy continues, "as if all of the dynamics of human relationships and intergenerational contact are reinscribed within this contained self, and as if the family—itself a certain erasure of the social and of the community in the contemporary United States—could now be fully privatized and enclosed within the individual."[15]

Inner-child therapies, according to Ivy, deflect attention from the ongoing neglect of real children in the most affluent nation of the world, where one of every five children lives in poverty. The addictive-compulsive behavior that these therapies seek to address is in no small measure engendered by consumer culture itself. Consumer culture feeds into feelings of inadequacy, low self-esteem, and envy, creating, as Stuart and Elizabeth Ewen have described in *Channels of Desire*, an insatiable thirst for fulfillment through commodities—fulfillment that is ever elusive because it thrives on an image-based culture of consumption that renders a thing obsolete as soon as one has bought it.

Drawing upon the work of socialist feminists, particularly Michelle Barrett and Mary McIntosh in *The Anti-social Family*, Ivy characterizes the family itself as antisocial, in that it is constructed as a private sphere outside capitalist relations and therefore is called upon to absorb the crises of alienated life generated by the market. It is only under capitalism that the family, imagined as its Other, is constructed as a noneconomic site. However, the ability of the family to absorb the ravages of capital was drastically reduced by the end of the twentieth century, beginning with—as Stephen Resnick and Richard Wolff discuss in "The Reagan-Bush Strategy"—the Reagan-Bush policy of advancing private enterprise by shifting social welfare (the care of the sick, the elderly, and children) onto the family; at the same time, the ability of the family to provide such care has been crushed by job loss, falling wages, and the need for both parents to work. Feminism itself has played an ambiguous part in this collapse of the family, as Arlie Hochschild has forcefully argued, by the ideology of self-advancement and self-management. Bourgeois feminism has translated itself into a disinvestment from emotional attachments in the pursuit of market-defined individualist success.[16]

Finally, at the apex of the capitalist regime of more than two centuries stands the privatized bourgeois individual, who is called upon to assume within his or her lonesome self the care once given and received among family members. This is quite similar to the common strain in commercials that invites us to buy a gift for ourselves, whether it is a perfume, a car, or a cooking gadget. Gift giving is reduced from an exchange between people to a solitary relationship between the individual and commodities.

However, it would be a mistake to assume that capital succeeds in completely subsuming the breakdown of the walls between childhood and adulthood into a thirst for market-produced commodities. If that were the case, there would be no cultural war over what it means to be young, a war that can be read in the contradictions that abound in children's texts such as *Jumanji*. For *Jumanji* wrestles with what it means to be able to go backward and forward in time and the new possibilities this offers for the young and the old.

The notions of childhood and adulthood, after all, are based on a notion of time, which is linear, that is, it has an origin and an end. As Hugh Cunningham, a historian, has pointed out in *Children and Childhood*, the notion of childhood represents a particularly modernist worldview in which childhood/savagery was seen as leading to adulthood/civilization. Similarly, psychoanalysis seeks to understand the causes of adult neurosis in childhood trauma, while Marx understood the present as an unstable condition arising out of the historical contest between the means of production—the technical apparatus held by a social formation and the relations of production—or, in other words, the state of the class struggle. Both psychoanalysis and Marxism understand that the present is an outcome of human and social production, not a divine or satanic invention.

At first glance, it appears that *Jumanji*'s explorations of time are remarkably similar to inner-child therapy's privatized bourgeois discourse and therefore a cynical appropriation of childhood by adults in the service of individual gratification. However, in casting children as the protagonists who valiantly go forth to meet the future, the film creates a narrative that immensely empowers children and suggests to adults that the future can be different from the present.

The permeability of the past and future is not limited to new technologies and consumer culture alone but, as Stephen Hawking tells us in *A Brief History of Time*, represents an accepted notion in the quantum physics idea of imaginary time as well. In imaginary time, it is possible to go into the future and then return, just as one can move south in geographical space and then turn right back. Translated into real time, it would mean, according to Hawking, that we would be able to remember the future, live our life backward and die before we were born, and get younger with time, and that effects would precede causes. It would be as if life could rewind like a film. We would be able to see, Hawking gives as an example, broken pieces gather themselves back into a cup and jump back on the table. For a generation that has cut its teeth on time-altering nonlinear technologies like television, video, and the Internet, it is not a leap to imagine that time does not move in one direction alone.

What is at stake in this play with time is the desire to control, predict, and shape the future. The discovery of the future—the title of H. G. Wells's remarkable 1902 essay—is at least a century and half old, as socialists, capitalists, artists, scientists, and writers have increasingly come to justify their present actions by measuring them against a possible future rather than against the past.[17] This process only became more radicalized by the late twentieth century when, as Fredric Jameson reminds us, the present was defamiliarized by being linked to an unspecified future rather than to a historical past, to the degree that the present appears as a memory or reconstruction.[18] The present then becomes a sphere of action. The logic is quite simple: If we do not act now, this is what awaits us. Released in 1995, *Jumanji* presents two alternative scenarios for that year—either chaotic disintegration as a children's game runs amok, or an orderly existence in which adults take on the responsibility for raising children. The resolution does reinstate the patriarchal bourgeois family, but it is in the difficulty with which it is obtained that we see the profound disorientation that results from children's integration into consumer society amidst the crumbling privatized space of the bourgeois family.

Adults as History's Dropouts

In a fundamental departure from Van Allsburg's book, the film *Jumanji* is very much directed toward adults, even displacing the children, Peter and Judy, to secondary roles in comparison with the adults, Alan and Sarah. Alan Parrish has spent the last twenty-six years lost in the land of Jumanji, while Sarah has spent those years in various kinds of therapy, including trying to imagine Alan as a radiant light, trying to forget her childhood encounter with Jumanji. Thus the game, akin to inner-child therapies, becomes a metaphor for the incomplete business of childhood fears and anxieties; likewise, finishing the game is imperative to becoming effective adults.

Similar to the adults in *Matilda*, *Home Alone*, and *Toy Story*, the adults in *Jumanji* are failures. They are presented as historical dropouts who have shirked their responsibilities toward their children, spending their lives instead dealing with inner monsters. The narrative of progress is given up in this late twentieth-century rendering of the Rip Van Winkle tale. While Rip Van Winkle slept for twenty years and awoke to find that a republic had replaced the monarchy, Alan Parrish finds small-town America turned into an inner-city ghetto. All of the earlier symbols of authority—his father, his father's factory, which he ran as a tight ship, and the clean and orderly rows of houses and streets—have given way to signs of urban decay. Graffiti lines the walls, stores are closing out, and homeless people stand in the streets.

The ineffectiveness of the adults is made to extend beyond Alan and Sarah to the entire generation. Peter and Judy's aunt, overwhelmed by the responsibilities of raising two children by herself, plays over and over again a tape that tells her that everything is under control. When she opens her eyes after reciting this mantra, she sees a stampede of animals right in front of her car, with a snorting baby dinosaur bringing up the rear. The joke is on adults who are so paralyzed by their inner fears—fears that they should have laid to rest in their childhood—that they are unable to act upon an external world that is rapidly disintegrating into chaos.

Characterizing the sixties as a time of historical dropping out is a disingenuous move, because that generation hardly dropped out of history. Rather, it actively intervened in history by refusing to play along, protesting not only U.S. imperialism and class but also race and gender inequities. This period is characterized in the film as one of self-indulgent fads rather than of resistance. Alan, who comes out of the game looking like a hippy, with a long beard and leaves around his waist, is variously explained by the kids as a vegetarian or a Peace Corps volunteer who has just returned from Indonesia. However, it is also true that many of the sixties generation gave into fads geared toward remaining young and individualist lifestyle solutions rather than participate in collective struggles for social transformation.

Thus, left to their own devices, the children unleash a chaotic world, which in keeping with the film's PG rating is a toned-down version of dystopic images that currently abound in the adult sci-fi genre. Upon seeing people and wild animals running wild in the marketplace, Peter asks Sarah what might be going on, and she replies, "Must be a sale." The monkeys that had come out of the game join the throngs that are looting the shops. They stop to watch a video game being played on a monitor in a show window as if looking at their own reflection in a mirror. Here primitive childhood fears of abandonment in a hostile world mirror the frightening world of late twentieth-century consumer culture, as children fear being crushed under a stampede of wild ancient animals and shoppers gone crazy.

These scenes in which the private fantasies unleashed by the game erupt into the public space would seem to validate Baudrillard's claims that the social realm we occupy is already a simulation through and

6.1. and 6.2. The postindustrial landscape is one in which the primitive commingle with the remnants of late consumer culture.

through. We don't need gloves or a digital suit to experience virtual reality since, he claims, we are already "moving around in the world as in a synthesized image."[19] We are condemned to live in the world of images, where our inner ones feed on the outer ones and vice versa in an endless stream from which there is no escape. Furthermore, one suspects that for Baudrillard there is no particular reason to try and find an escape. However, in opposition to Baudrillard's almost fascinated celebration of the end of human agency, *Jumanji* presents children both as the reason for and the agents who look under the spectacle to reclaim the present as something worth fighting for.

The Children's Struggle

In sharp contrast to the adults, the children in *Jumanji* are shown to have remarkable confidence and sense of purpose. It is Peter and Judy who repeatedly bring Sarah and Alan back into the game—sometimes manipulating them, other times cajoling them—and succeed in completing it. They bring up the adults to accept life, including the death of one's parents. During one of his many refusals to go on with the game, Alan stands before his father's grave while Peter consoles him, telling him that his own parents too are dead, and succeeds in bringing him back to finish the game.

Similar to *Toy Story* and *Matilda*, the film parodies the notion that children are innocents, showing them instead to be very capable of seeing through and manipulating adults' hackneyed ideas about children. At one point in the film, Peter lures Alan back into Jumanji by claiming that Alan is too afraid to join the game. "It is all right to be afraid," he tells Alan understandingly, which provokes Alan into continuing with the game to prove that he is not afraid. Peter then tells Judy that he was simply practicing "reverse psychology," just like his father used to with him. In another sequence, Judy has a laugh at the expense of the realtor selling her aunt the house by telling her a cock-and-bull story of how she and her brother were abused by their parents. As the realtor puts on a face of acute sympathy, Judy walks away, barely suppressing her laughter.

Both the book and the film reiterate the motif common to children's texts at the end of the twentieth century that children have to depend upon themselves to get out of the troubles that face them. There are no strong adults, no mother or father, who will take control and chase away the nightmare. In the book, when Peter asks Judy to call the zoo to take away a lion, she replies: "No one would come from the zoo because they would not believe us. . . . We started this game and now we have to finish it." The film pushes this notion even further. Peter and Judy must finish not only a game they started but also one started by their parents' generation. To reclaim their childhood, they have first to raise their parents into adulthood. In this way, the film moves a step ahead—or should we say back—from Matilda, who is responsible only for raising herself, not her imbecilic parents.

Childhood's New Image

Like the newer films made for children, *Jumanji* parodies older modes of childhood and the rigid boundaries between adulthood and childhood. While *Matilda* plays with the horror-film genre, *Jumanji* pokes fun at safe and dull children's board games. Childhood is presented as a state of confinement rather than of idyllic bliss by contrasting the limitations of the private world of the family with the unlimited world of children's imaginations. Peter and Judy's compulsive storytelling, their lies and exaggerations, are made understandable by setting them against the confining limits of innocent childhood.

In speaking of childhood as a prison house, the film takes up, albeit rather tentatively, the issue of children's sexuality. Once the game is finished, it is time for Sarah and Alan to turn back into children, and they confront the question of what a return to childhood would be like. Instead of the unmitigated return to paradise suggested by romantic notions of childhood, the return is viewed with some regret. Sarah, for all of her ineffectiveness as an adult, expresses regret at having to forget what it was like to be an adult—that is, to be sexual. She then kisses Alan, saying she wants to do that before "I forget and feel like a kid." Children are still presented as asexual. However, in a remarkable retake of the Garden of Eden myth, childhood can be acquired even after the kiss. This acknowledgment of children's sexuality, for all its timidity and more than a century after Freud, nevertheless signals a progressive acknowledgment of children as sexual and therefore fully human.

Of course, the monsoons, the tropical forests, and the floods in the house can all be interpreted as unconscious sexual desires unleashed by bored children left unsupervised one afternoon. These are even more threatening because they are assumed to be primitive and unruly, since they come out of children's heads. All the fantastic happenings unleashed by the game are ascribed to an imagined African jungle with species that are already extinct, such as gigantic bats, dinosaurs, and giant mosquitoes. They are let loose by children of at least three generations, assuming here an essential continuity between children. For instance, when Judy and Peter claim that they saw bats in the attic and show pictures of them to the man who comes to check the house, he replies that another child had reported seeing the same bats in the sixties but that they are a species long extinct. At the same time the film ventures forth an acknowledgment of children as knowledgeable about sexuality, it ultimately sees children's sexuality as potentially dangerous.

The Lessons of Consumer Culture

Ultimately, the film restores order through the reinstatement of the nuclear family. Alan and Sarah get married and have children of their own. Alan has reconciled with his father, who has shifted from being an authority figure to being an affectionate one. Alan has also "grown up" and taken over his father's property. He now runs the family business and has employed Peter and Judy's father. Alan and Sarah succeed in averting the death of Peter and Judy's parents by refusing to grant leave to their father to go on the vacation on which he and their mother had died in the future. Thus, adults are restored as knowing figures, private property is restored, and vacations are abolished as irresponsible forays from the higher purpose of running the family business.

The final lesson the children must learn, as in *Toy Story*, is to be proper consumers, for as this film indicates, children's boredom and unlimited curiosity threaten not only the family but also businesses. The game comes with these directions written in capitals: "VERY IMPORTANT. ONCE A GAME OF JUMANJI IS STARTED IT WILL NOT BE OVER UNTIL ONE PLAYER REACHES THE GOLDEN CITY." And true to its words, once started, the game moves on its own. The children try to find explanations for this in the technology appropriate to their generation. Peter and Judy believe that the self-moving capability of the game is made possible by a microchip, while Alan and Sarah think that the game must be magnetized.

Here play is not imagined as a process of self-realization. Instead, it is an example of what Marx theorized as the fetishism of commodities, or the "topsy-turvy" world in which the human is replaced by the nonhuman and all the things that you cannot do, your money can do. "It can eat and drink, go to the dance hall and the theater; it can travel, it can appropriate art, learning, the treasures of the past, political power—all this it can appropriate for you—it can buy all this for you."[20]

The game in this case, like the toys in *Toy Story*, comes alive and wields power over children. The only way out is to play by its rules, rules that are set not by the children or the parents but by the toy manufacturer. The dangers of not following the rules are made chillingly clear in the book. As Peter and Judy look out their window, they see their neighbor's children, Daniel and Walter, run away with the game, which Peter and Judy had thrown out of the house. The neighbor mother, who is at Peter and Judy's house for dinner, says at that very moment: "Daniel and Walter are always starting puzzles and never finishing them. They never read instructions, either." We are left to imagine the horrors that will befall poor Daniel and Walter, a cautionary lesson here to middle-class children of the dangers that will befall them if they do not read instructions or follow rules.

These contemporary children's texts serve to socialize children into the world of commodity culture as docile adults by impressing upon them the lesson that they must follow rules even in their play. The consequences of not following rules, children are taught, would be a nightmarish world from which they would have to extricate themselves without any help from adults or any leeway given to them because they are children—a bitter lesson in bourgeois self-reliance aimed at adjusting children at an early age to a world in which the other, including the adult, is imagined not as a caregiver or fellow traveler but as a competitor and antagonist.

The contradictions of *Jumanji*, its celebration and anxiety around the erosion of adult-child polarity, reflects the societal contest over the meaning of childhood, which ultimately is a struggle over the meaning of what it is to be human. The film at once sympathizes with the boredom inherent in the state of childhood and issues warnings against it. It is a protest against consumer culture and also its reinstatement. Nevertheless, there is one unambiguous element in the film's deconstruction of childhood: Children are imagined as capable of taking care of themselves and the adults in their lives. These postmodern children raise the adults and wrestle with the future, turning it from certain decay to order. Children, like everyone else in capital, are made responsible for their own lives, including the future.

However, to respond by attempting to put children back into the mold of innocent dependents not only is unrealistic but also will be resisted by our children. Instead, we should take up consumer culture's promises to children that they can be protagonists of history by making them our allies in our collective struggles. The child needs to experience that the present can be acted upon in solidarity with others by standing in peace vigils, joining demonstrations, and taking part in other activist interventions. It is through this active engagement with the world that children become persons and intuit socialism—that is, live the nonalienated life in community with others.

7

Free Market, Branded Imagination

Harry Potter and the Commercialization of Children's Culture

Harry had never been to London before. Although Hagrid seemed to know where he was going, he was obviously not used to getting there in the ordinary way. . . . "I don't know how the Muggles manage without magic," he said.

—J. K. Rowling,
Harry Potter and the Sorcerer's Stone

Just when it seemed that magic had become passé even in its last home, children's culture, along came J. K Rowling's *Harry Potter and the Sorcerer's Stone* and the 2001 film made from the book and directed by Chris Columbus.[1] After all, children's mass culture in the late twentieth century derived a great deal of merriment from ridiculing the idea of magic as the old-fashioned ingredient of nineteenth-century children's tales, now simply too tame—and should we say, childish?—for a generation that cut its teeth on video games and marketing campaigns designed to address them as a niche market. Now mainstream films like *Toy Story* (1995) made for general consumption mocked the idea that stories of toys coming to life had to be imbued with mystery. When the toys came to life in this film they asked: "Are you from Mattel?" "Were you made in Hong Kong?" Toothpaste commercials deconstruct the tooth fairy by casting a man in drag as the tooth fairy. In a commercial for Disneyland and Visa credit cards, the child cajoles its parents, putting on an "innocent" face, to make purchases with the card so that they can win a trip to Disneyland.

In contrast, Harry Potter, an orphan who is left to the mercy of his upwardly mobile suburban aunt, uncle, and cousin, finds out one day that he is a wizard. He also finds out that there is an entire world, a way of life with its own language and culture, that lives by magic and coexists parallel to the world of the "Muggles," the wizards' term for the "normal," routine-bound, monotonous, magicless everyday world. Did the film *Harry Potter and the Sorcerer's Stone*, then, indicate a return of the utopian imagination in children's cinema? Not quite. Instead, Harry Potter is an excellent lesson about the limits of fantasy when it is produced as a commodity driven by an industry continuously raising the stakes for a film's survival in terms of the returns expected from it.

The limits of the utopian imagination obvious in the film's aesthetics stem from the Mugglish political-economic realities of the business of film production at the end of the twentieth century. Ultimately, we must ask a question as old as capitalism itself: What is the nature of the magic that the market serves its consumers? The cornerstone of the free-market ideology espoused by Hollywood is the notion that it is not its producers but its consumers who make a film. What kind of magic wand could create such a vision? To fully unravel this riddle, it is important to historically trace the selling of Harry Potter and the transformation it underwent from a book not written as a film-to-be into a franchise or a pretext for selling other market-produced commodities.

In a rave review in *Variety*, Todd McCarthy reiterates the magic mantra that makes us responsible for the films we get: "For tens of millions of fans the world over who have taken J.K. Rowling's marvelously imaginative novel (and its three sequels thus far) to their hearts, Warner Bros. smartly produced and elaborately manufactured $125 million-plus visualization will essentially make their dreams come true." McCarthy goes on to enumerate the efforts made by the producers to serve the audience exactly what it wanted. According to him, the producers adhered as closely as possible to the text, hiring a director who would "obediently serve the material" without any danger of "idiosyncratic flights of fancy" that a more "high-powered and personal filmmaker (such as Steven Spielberg or Terry Gilliam)" would indulge in. The result, in McCarthy's own assessment, is a film that "never takes on a life or soul of its own," which nevertheless "will have no bearing on how many times youngsters and even adults will return to this high flying entertainment that looks poised to become one of the biggest-grossing films of all time."[2]

While this review was published in *Variety*, a trade journal, the evaluation of a film according to its box-office returns has become a regular aspect of journalistic film reviews. The phenomenon started in 1976, as Fredrick Wasser reports, with a small company called Entertainment Data, Inc (EDI), which started to report box-office returns from participating theaters.[3] By the 1980s, EDI reports included about 80 percent of the nation's theaters. Quick, accurate reporting fed the growing trend in mainstream newspapers, such as the *New York Times*, to report box-office figures as news. That a film's critical review should partly be based on its costs and revenue is symptomatic of the blurring of commerce and culture.

The children's-film genre has been at the forefront of the commercialization of culture, of the construction of "consumption webs" such that media (film being one) and other commodities constantly advertise each other. A film is launched as an "event" designed to sell not only the movie, but also toys, clothes, videos, record albums, and computer games, and to attract so much attention that one would have to live in another world to escape these commodities. A glance at the most successful high-concept or event films of the 1990s shows the overwhelming importance of the children's or family film in this category: *Home Alone* and *Ghost* (1990), *Aladdin* (1992), *The Lost World: Jurassic Park* (1993), *The Lion King* (1994), and *Titanic* (1997).

Since the high-concept film is, as Justin Wyatt has argued in *High Concept*, a marketing concept, it is designed to maximize returns by eliminating ambiguity in favor of easy recognizability (through dependence on stars or genre) and simple narratives (stock situations, simplification of character and plot) that can be translated across a wide range of commodities. In "The Magical Market of Disney," Janet Wasko characterizes this phenomenon as "cultural synergy." Accordingly, in the preproduction stage, the film is conceived of as a brand, that is, companies promote their activities across a growing number of outlets that can be cross-promoted and then distributed through media conglomerates across a range of media. Understanding the bounds this places on the utopian imagination in children's culture is the key to understanding the confines of the role of the consumer in a cultural environment dominated by the centralization of media ownership and the convergence of media culture and other forms of commodity culture.

Of Movies and Muggles: The Political Economy of the Event Film

While the basic logic of commercial filmmaking has remained the same—to minimize production costs and maximize profits—the nature of the business has changed because of the media mergers of the late twentieth century and new technologies such as television, VCRs, and the Internet. Janet Staiger and Justin Wyatt have shown how the changes in ownership of the industry have increased the costs and therefore the risks of the movies business. According to Janet Staiger in "The Package-Unit System," the shift from the studio system toward the package-unit system of film production—a producer organizes a film project, secures financing, and combines the necessary workers (actors, director, music composer, etc.) and physical elements (screenplay, sets, etc.)—has increased the economic risk because these commercial ventures do not have the safety net provided by the studios in the past. Moreover, studios now function as distributors rather than producers and are more likely to pick up projects that promise minimum risk.

Further, studios no longer exist as independent entities but as part of media conglomerates that have interests in television, the Internet, journalism, the recording industry, and cable. Consequently, media conglomerates seek to balance risk among their various subsidiaries and are more likely to pick up projects that can cross over these various media and ancillary markets. Wyatt has also highlighted the dependence on market research, particularly of the quantitative and empirical kind, within media conglomerates in deciding which film projects get made. These marketing executives, who tend to come primarily from advertising, rely on market-research models developed for the sale of packaged goods and merchandize. This reliance on quantifiable data makes it difficult to appreciate projects that are more innovative and complex and that emphasize the visual or aural (rather than narrative) aspects of cinema.

The tendency to favor blockbuster treatments is also an outcome of changes in distribution since the seventies, with the initiation of "four walling," a system ironically pioneered by a low-budget film, *Billy Jack* (1971). The basic principle was to intensely promote the film in all possible channels and saturate the market so that there would be high public awareness for the film's opening weekend. The strategy included leasing all the theaters in a particular region and advertising on television. This process has continued at a national level, driven by the objective to pack in audiences the first week to reduce the risk of losing audiences on account of poor word-of-mouth.

This strategy is driven by an economic logic, Dan Ackman writes, according to which studios take 70 percent of a film's total box-office receipts in the first week of its release.[4] The studio's percentage is generally reduced to about 30 percent in the succeeding weeks. This has further raised the stakes for creating awareness of a film before its release. Fredrick Wasser cites Motion Picture Association of America figures to show that while U.S. spending on advertising increased significantly in the years 1981–1994, movie advertising grew at nearly twice that rate.[5] These increased costs have further diminished the economic risks producers are willing to take with film projects.

Harry Potter and the Sorcerer's Stone set a box-office record in the first three days of its release, earning $93.5 million in ticket sales, according to studio estimates.[6] This surpassed the three-day record set by *The Lost World: Jurassic Park* in 1997 of $72.1 million. The success owes itself to the marketing of the film and the practice of saturating the market in the first week of a film's release. The movie opened in 3,672 theaters on 8,200 screens, about one of every four screens in the United States, with most theaters playing *Potter* on more than one screen. In contrast, *Star Wars: Episode 1—The Phantom Menace* had played only on about 5,000 screens in its opening weekend, for which it raked in $65 million.[7]

Moreover, Harry Potter was already a household name by the time of the film's release. It had a major presold component: the book. Time Warner had optioned the book shortly after its British publication in 1997 but before it became a smash hit. Since then, Harry Potter was planned as a franchise. Consequently, it is difficult to separate the success of the book sequels and their continued performance as number one on Amazon from the marketing campaigns that surrounded them. The books were released with elaborate marketing campaigns designed as hide-and-seek games between consumers and book retailers.

The fourth book in the series, *Harry Potter and the Goblet of Fire*, was released amidst a highly publicized secret campaign. Warehouses were bristling with security. Booksellers were forbidden to unpack books before midnight of the release date, while at the same time publishing records were noisily broadcast: 3.8 million first copies printed in the United States and a million more in Britain. Amazon promised Saturday delivery for the first fifty thousand book orders. Even Amazon's contract with the Fed Ex Corporation became part of the advertising campaign, with the shipping company calling the order the "largest single day distribution event in the history of business to consumer e-commerce."[8] Not to be outdone, Barnesandnoble.com too promised Saturday delivery for orders placed by Friday at 11 A.M.

The same marketing strategy built around suspense was played out during the release of the fifth book in the series. J. K Rowling and her publishers sued Reuters News Agency for reporting on some details from the book before its release. The reasons for the secrecy lie in the logic of the event film, now brought to children's literature. Keeping a single date for the book's release builds anticipation, forestalls any loss in sales due to poor word-of-mouth that follows the book, and is a strategy that can be sustained by the large chain stores that own the book business. These large chains can centralize marketing strategy and synchronize release; one outcome of this centralization is to weaken competition among booksellers.

Bookstores planned Harry Potter parties and other gimmicks to lure customers, including opening at midnight. On the morning of the book's release, media lined up to interview those waiting to buy the books, sometimes equaling or outnumbering the buyers. The release was planned as an event that included photo opportunities for adults and children to pose in Harry Potter garb. This hype continued with the release of the film. In Carbondale, Illinois, where I live, children and adults came to the film in Harry Potter garb and could have their photos taken before the screening.

The time between the release of the fourth book and the release of the fifth was filled with two quick spin-offs of the book itself, Rowling's *Quidditch through the Ages* and *Fantastic Beasts and Where to Find Them*. Reviews on Amazon were already claiming that these slim books, marketed to look like Hogwarts textbooks annotated with Harry's comments, would become collectors' items. Both are written in the dull style of school textbooks, and their appeal can be explained only as a result of advertising, the self-selection of Harry Potter fans into a subculture in which the history of Quidditch becomes a lingua franca, and the widespread acknowledgment of the commodification of childhood nostalgia such that children are encouraged to buy with a future collectibles market in mind.

Besides the book, there were other aspects of commodity culture used to prepare the audience for the release of the film. Promotions for computer and video games were afoot in July 2000, almost sixteen months before the film's release. Electronic Arts acquired the license to develop these games and claimed that it was working closely with Christopher Columbus and J. K. Rowling. In the year 1999, Electronic Arts had signed a five-year agreement with AOL to deliver online games and interactive entertainment for AOL's nineteen million users. The merger of AOL and Time Warner provided Electronic Arts the opportunity to piggyback on Potter's name, already in circulation.

The film was widely advertised on the media subsidiaries held by AOL Time Warner, such as its television channels—WB, Cartoon Network, and CNN. Its magazines, including *Time, Entertainment Weekly*, and *People*, carried articles on the movie and Rowling. Rowling's personal story—that she was a single mom struggling on welfare when she wrote the book—was exactly the kind of rags-to-riches tale so favored by capitalism. *Time* magazine, including its children's section, had been carrying articles on Harry Potter, including a cover story titled "Wild about Harry," way back in its September 20, 1999, issue, shortly after the book had been optioned for film.

Typical of other commercial children's films, Harry Potter found its way into other forms of children's commodity culture. Mattel held the license for Harry Potter toys. It sold action figures that ranged in price from $9.99 for the smaller plastic figures to $119 for the larger ones, such as Harry Potter battling the mountain troll. Tiger Electronics, also under license, produced alarm clocks with talking portraits inspired by the moving portraits in the film, and a book of spells. Other paraphernalia included a Harry Potter Trivia game, a board game, costumes, and puzzles. Scholastic Paperbacks, the publisher of the Harry Potter series, came out with Harry Potter journals, a stationery kit, and even Hogwarts crests. By the time of the film's release, the marketing Muggles had ensured that only those in a comatose state had not heard of Harry Potter.

How the Muggles Stole Fantasy

Todd McCarthy's review in *Variety*, cited earlier, made no connection between the blockbuster nature of the film and what McCarthy admits is a text that "lacks a soul." This soullessness (or homogenization, to be more accurate) is grounded in the political-economic realities of branding, which is a further development of the idea of the high-concept or event film. The high-concept idea, Fredrick Wasser indicates in V*eni, Vidi, Video*, was the brainchild of Barry Diller at ABC, who demanded film projects that could be easily summarized in both the abbreviated thirty-second television commercial and in the sentence synopsis of *TV Guide*. It is entirely logical that this commercialized cultural form should come out of television, which from its inception had been required to grab viewer attention in brief fragments to sell products.

At the core of the branding strategy is the need for an easy summary. Any degree of complexity creates confusion and therefore difficulty in sustaining a brand image. As Naomi Klein explains in *No Logo*, the success of a branding strategy, driven by synergy, depends upon repetition and visibility. The correct way to imagine a brand, as Janet Wasko suggests in *The Magical Market of Disney*, is to think of it as the axis of a wheel, whose spokes branch out into various products, all designed to repeat the brand image. Harry Potter as a gay icon, for example, would be problematic (it would introduce conflicts), while reducing magic to a series of special effects would be entirely compatible with a marketing strategy aimed at reducing complexity.[9] Films built around branding strategies, therefore, have the textual complexity of a commercial or a movie trailer.

In fact, similar to commercials, one of the most exciting human activities presented in *Harry Potter and the Sorcerer's Stone* is shopping. Aspiring wizards and witches press their noses against a show window, eyeing with longing the latest branded broomstick on display, the Nimbus 2000. The camera pans (to a sigh of the desiring children) in the style of commercials to reveal the brand name, not only in the show window but also later when Harry receives the broomstick as a gift for Christmas. Like children's candy on store shelves today, Bertie Bott's Every Flavor Beans comes in a "variety of disgusting flavors," and like the promotional toys that induce children to eat at McDonald's, chocolate frogs in the wizard world are bought for the holographic cards that come with them.

The taming of the utopian imagination in fantasy produced for mass marketing is most obvious in the transformation of Rowling's book into a franchise. While the book presents a parody of the privatized bourgeois family wrapped up in consumer culture, that critical element is totally absent from the film. I am not suggesting that the entire

7.1. Aspiring wizards eye the broom in the shop window.

7.2. The camera pans to reveal the brand name.

book is an unmitigated critique of consumer society, rather that critical elements in the book are elided in the simplistic treatment given it by the film.

The element of magic that so appealed to the book's readers was premised upon the contrast Rowling sets up between the wizards and the Muggles by dwelling considerably on the privatized, routine life of the Dursleys. Contrary to the film's quick and efficient dismissal of Harry's stay with them as a poor stepchild, Rowling's account dwells on the contrast between Harry and the Dursleys' pampered and greedy son, Dudley. Rowling describes Mr. Dursley as a "large beefy man with

7.3. Harry receives a birthday gift.

7.4. The children can't wait for Harry to open his gift.

hardly any neck" who is the director of a big firm that makes drills. His wife, thin and blond, "had the usual amount of neck, which came in very useful as she spent so much of her time craning over garden fences, spying on the neighbors."[10]

The family is marked by an intense desire to be "normal," fears any diversity, and is obsessed with minding their own "business," which for Mrs. Dursley is keeping her home and for Mr. Dursley, selling

7.5. Harry's gift is none other than a Nimbus 2000.

drills. The Dursleys' biggest fear is that their neighbors will come to know that Mrs. Dursley's sister, Harry's mother, was a witch, making them stand out in a typical suburban neighborhood whose neat rows of houses have nothing out of place. In Rowling's text, the "normalcy" that the Dursleys desire is the exact opposite of imagination. Of Mr. Dursley's plight upon encountering wizards on the streets, including being hugged by a complete stranger in a cloak, Rowling writes: "He hurried to his car and set off for home, hoping he was imagining things, which he had never hoped before, because he didn't approve of imagination" (5).

The Dursleys spend all their energies on their son, lavishing him with gifts, which on his birthday include a racing bike, a video camera, a remote-control car, sixteen new computer games, and a VCR. Moreover, all the gifts are wrapped. When Dudley objects that he has only thirty-six presents, one short of the previous year's total, Mr. Dursley responds: "Little tyke wants his money's worth, just like his father" (22). Dudley, a bully and always greedy for more, is seen "kicking his mother all the way up the street, screaming for sweets" (13). In fact, the book can be read as a modern-day socializing tale from a mother to a child, warning of the impossibility of finding happiness in market-produced commodities. By painting a picture of the consuming child as whiny, fat, and unlikable, Rowling caricatures the child consumer as a spoiled brat who has lost his imagination.

The film sidesteps Rowling's caricature of the privatized bourgeois family by making Hogwarts, the wizard school, the center of the story.

What it sells through Hogwarts is Englishness evoked as a class symbol, following a tradition in children's literature, particularly in North America and India. No alternative school, Hogwarts is in every way constructed to uphold the elitism of the British private school, where the usual stereotypes of race and gender prevail. The power of money stays intact in the school. Before they can enter this elite institution, children must acquire books, uniforms, and supplies (wands, in this case) that require a rather large sum of money and reflect their class backgrounds. Harry Potter is left a locker filled with gold by his parents, and he shares his wealth with Ron Weasley, one of five children, whom everyone in the school understands to be poor. Teachers are authoritative and relations among students marked by hierarchy and competition. The children are in awe and fear of Albus Dumbledore, Professor McGonagall, and Snape, all of whom are referred to as professors, wear cloaks when teaching, and sit at the high table in the dining hall.

The choice of locations and stars banked on selling Englishness as a commodity. A twelfth-century castle on the Scottish border, Alnwick, was cast as Hogwarts; a tenth-century Anglican cathedral located in Gloucestershire as the entrance to Gryffindor Hall, Harry's dormitory; and the elaborate banquet scenes staged on a sound set made to replicate the dining hall of Oxford University's largest college. In this day and age of spin-offs, the British Tourist Authority issued a Harry Potter movie map (available at www.travelbritain.com) that details sites open to visitors. The 150-year-old London Rail station was marked with signs such as "No spells on platforms," "Owls must be caged at all times," and "No Broom Parking" to direct visitors to platform $9^3/_4$, the Hogwarts train stop.

The special effects, location, or casting are in a highly commercial film not an integral part of the narrative but the narrative itself, which is little more than a series of events strung together like movie trailers. From the Quidditch match to adventures with the troll to the final confrontation with Voldemort, the narrative is at best a mystery story, with none of the mythic qualities of transformation. The mise-en-scène is so taken up with rendering magic in the most realistic way possible that it has no connection with developing or revealing the inner psychological states of the film's characters and becomes an end in itself.

This literal rendering of magic trivializes fantasy, reducing it to a spectacle characteristic of video games. For instance, at Hogwarts pictures talk, ghosts roam freely, and staircases move by themselves. While they can quite simply be a feature of a wizard's school, these phenomena can also express the fears and anxieties of finding one's way around the overpowering environs of institutions where traditions seem to have a life of their own and are founded upon making a child feel small enough to want to conform. However, by presenting these simply as aspects of the school and not as a child's perception of them, the film turns them into mechanical devices that can be mastered, not unlike elevators or doors that children must learn to traverse.

This fetishization of technology, which comes to stand in for the absence of content, was amply in evidence in the film's self-promotion. David Heyman boasted in an article by Jess Cagle in the November 5, 2001, issue of *Time* that the primary costs of the film would be in the special effects: "We want to make all of that as believable and fantastical as possible. Technology is now incredible."

In terms of race and gender, the status quo remains intact even in this magical school. The darker characters arouse suspicion. Professors Snape and Quirrell are both darker skinned; Quirrell even sports a turban. While the book has an Indian girl, Parvati Patel, in the school, the only noticeable student of color in the film is the young commentator during the Quidditch match. The wise and ancient centaur is cast distinctly as a black man. The goblins who guard Gringotts, the wizards' bank, are barely disguised Jewish stereotypes. Hermione Granger, Harry and Ron's girl pal, is presented as irritatingly smart and well-read.

The film's trivialization of fantasy is most blatant in the way in which the narrative sentimentalizes the notion of love. In the book, Harry learns through his life-threatening struggle with Voldemort that what had saved his life was his mother's love. She had died trying to save her son's life, and a life touched by a love like that is indestructible. While Voldemort could leave only a mark on Harry's forehead, Harry could with his bare hands turn to ash the body of Quirrell, now possessed by Voldemort. This is a powerful fantasy of mythic proportions, but the film brings it to ground. Apparently, the lessons the children learn about friendship, intelligence, and love are not enough in themselves. What is more important for the film's closure is the contest for the house cup. The film ends with the school principal, Albus Dumbledore, announcing the victory of Harry's house, setting the stage for the sequel and casting the series as a set of stories about a British boarding school and not a fantasy about another world.

How then are we to understand the enthusiasm generated by the film as a magical phenomenon that both adults and children were flocking to pay money to see? Part of the answer lies in the marketing of the film and its self-promotion as fantasy. The other part lies in our desire to see magic, particularly in children's culture. The crowds that the film attracted in the first days was the result of the two years of marketing and also the events of September 11 and later, which made fantasy desirable, perhaps as a way to forget but also as a way to find hope. The film also provided a venue for parents and children to come together and share a cultural experience. There was generally an atmosphere of happy expectation around the film screenings, making the film a family event or a collective experience. The photo opportunities added to this sense of the film as a community event.

Since large numbers of the audience, both children and adults, knew the book, watching the film became an active exercise as they compared the film to the book or, at the very least, followed the book through the course of the film. This comes to approximate folklore in our highly industrialized culture, in that we bring to these mass-produced stories our own versions and interact actively with them. Children spoke back at the film, predicting its narrative, and stayed after the show to discuss the film. Despite the film's limited imagination of Hogwarts as a private British elite school, the children I talked to had a more active understanding of it as a place where the adults were different from the "Muggles" they encountered in their own schools. The possibility that Hogwarts presents of growing up with other children and living a life of learning and curiosity with adults who are wise and filled with character (with magic tricks up their sleeves) is of course very appealing to children.

Children did not entirely "buy into" the film's selling of Harry Potter as a commodity but inserted themselves into it imaginatively. This is partly the reason why shelves filled with Harry Potter merchandise had finally to be cleared. There is a limit to how many Harry Potter objects a child wants to buy. Moreover, commodified fantasy is short-lived. Differentiated only by look and style, it is repetitive and minimal in content, easily replaced by another more spectacular commodity whose release is based on the planned obsolescence of the former. Just two months after the film's release, the shelves in the local Wal-Mart and Barnes and Noble had been cleared of Harry Potter merchandise. What remained had been dumped on the clearance shelves. The film had come and gone, with video release planned for May and a sequel the following year. How can the audience be responsible for what it sees when even its ability to watch is constrained by marketing strategies?

Even more revealing of the restrictions on mass-marketed fantasy was the bitter battle launched by AOL Time Warner against the Web sites held by fans of Harry Potter. AOL Time Warner issued letters of warning to fans, most of them teens and preteens, asking them to stop using the Harry Potter name. The first such letter was sent in December 2000 to fifteen-year-old Claire Field, asking that she take the domain name HarryPotterGuide.co.uk off her site and ending with this statement: "If we do not hear from you by 15 December 2000 we shall put this matter directly into the hands of our solicitors."[11]

In response, fans set up sites with wonderfully appropriate names like www.potterwar.org.uk. Other fans similarly threatened by Warner Brothers contacted them. These included Catherine Chang, a fifteen-year-old from Singapore who had already relinquished rights to her domain name www.thehpn.com; Sung Yoo, a twelve-year-old who was threatened for his site www.HarryPotterFAQ.com; and thirteen-year-olds Ross McCaw and Peter Walker regarding their site www.HarryPotterworld.com. A site held by the Defense Against the Dark Arts (DADA), *www.dprophet.com/dada* called for a boycott of all Potter merchandise except the books. They demanded that Warner Brothers pay reparations by making substantial donations to UNICEF and giving premiere tickets to fans they had threatened, to really "show how sorry they feel."

In the face of the bad publicity, Warner Brothers in March 2001 withdrew the threats of lawsuits. Nevertheless, the battle with corporate control over our children's imagination is not yet won. As www.potterwar.org.uk summarized, the withdrawal of legal action against fans is not a victory but "victor(-ish)." Warner Brothers did not return the domains they had taken, and more importantly, Harry Potter is only a battle in what promises to be a continuous war between corporations and fans.

The battle over Harry Potter's name clearly indicates the limits of fantasy branded by media corporations. Just as branding was originally a practice in which owners stamped cows with their names to mark them as private property, corporations are now engaged in claiming our imaginations. If it is true that we get the films we want, then why this contest over how we interpret these films? That the battle over our imaginations is not yet won is clear by the contradictory relationship media corporations have with fans. On the one hand, fans do the work of these corporations, buying their products and thus creating profits for them. On the other hand, when fans begin to create alternatives, they threaten the iron grip these corporations seek to retain on their brands. The true nature of the relationship between media corporations and audiences is revealed when the control of the former is threatened. Then, from posing as democrats who make what audiences want, these corporations transform into powerful policing agents.

In their letter to fans, Warner Brothers stated: "We are concerned that your domain name registration is likely to cause consumer confusion and dilution of the intellectual property rights."[12] Fantasy, in this view, clearly had one and only one purpose: to translate itself into consumer behavior. The Defense Against the Dark Arts characterized the threat this poses to our imagination quite aptly: "There are dark forces afoot, darker even than He-Who-Must-Not-Be-Named, because these dark forces are daring to take away something so basic, so human, that it's close to murder. They are taking away our freedom of speech, our freedom to express our thoughts, feelings and ideas, and they are taking away the fun of a magical book."[13]

In attempting to colonize children's imaginations, corporations reveal a fundamental truth about capitalism: No aspect of human life is left untouched in the search for profits. The desire to find magic in children's culture that got us into theaters in the first place speaks of our need to find an alternative, even utopian, imagination. That we think we can find it in children's culture speaks of a lingering social conception that childhood is distinctly different from adulthood, that from the site of childhood we can critique the inequities and injustices of this world and imagine a different one. However, the aggressive attempts by children's marketing to bring children into the market as consumers blurs that boundary.

Nevertheless, AOL Time Warner's battle with their fans reveals that victory over the human imagination is not easily won. Bringing children into the market as consumers can also politicize them against the market. We parents and older friends can either wring our hands at how corporations have taken the socializing of our children away from us, turning us into facilitators who must buy market-produced commodities to momentarily keep our kids from experiencing the anxiety, addiction, low self-esteem, and isolation so familiar to us as consumers (but in the long run turning them into adults who experience the same feelings). Or we can collaborate with our children in resisting the branding of our imaginations by refusing the most fantastic market-produced myth of all, the myth of choice, that is, that it is we who produce the products the market offers us.

Conclusion
All That is Solid Melts into Air

Childhood was the final frontier, the final niche
market to be captured by capital's incessant drive
to turn every aspect of our lives into a source of profit. I have argued
in this book that the invention of children as consumers brought down
the walls between childhood and adulthood. Its results are a growing
up of children as they are granted a certain recognition and autonomy
as consumers; a growing down of adults as they are promised youth
through the consumption of market-produced commodities; and the
commodification of childhood as it is no longer considered an inalien-
able attribute of children but the end product of consumer culture.
So we have children's movies that show children who have grown up,
adults who need help from children to grow up or are unable to grow
up, and children asked to raise themselves in the face of these ineffective adults. That these themes have moved from the sci-fi or horror genres into the children's or family film indicates that, from
rehearsing for the death of childhood, we now stand everywhere celebrating or mourning its demise.

Of course, this transformation is viewed with anxiety; tracing its
causes and contradictions has been the subject of this book. On the
religious Right there is the fear that children are growing up and out
of the patriarchal family, which the women misled by the women's
movement had already abandoned. The fears that *Harry Potter* is a satanic book or that the film *Pocahontas* has subliminal satanic messages

stem from the desire to keep children under the restraint of parental authority. The other block on the Right is comprised of neoliberal advocates and children's marketers who speak with forked tongues. While they are quick to announce that this generation of children is more grown up than any other and should therefore be given money to spend on its own, their advocacy of children's autonomy vanishes when confronted with children's interpretations that challenge their brand patents, as we saw in the case of AOL Time Warner's lawsuits against children who had their own Harry Potter Web sites.

Children's imagination, when not turned into a source for generating profit, becomes a terribly fearful thing that threatens to overturn the economic, sexual, and social status quo. The conservatives seek to tame the possibilities of autonomy (however limited) generated by the market and demand that the family curb its children, failing which are the state prisons. The underlying hostility to children is obvious in the casual way in which a harsh term like "zero tolerance" has become acceptable as a policy in relation to children. The market, represented in its purest form by neoliberal theory, collaborates, demanding that social welfare be abolished and individuals, including children, provide for themselves through their own effort and labor. The only childhood that capital can allow is sustained through the valiant efforts of adults who try to carve out within the private space of the family a gentler, loving enclave to raise children—an effort bound for tragedy because the privatized family is no match for capital.

The contribution of socialist-feminist theory today lies in the insights it can provide into the changing nature of the pact between capital and patriarchy, a theory that can inform political strategies of how to live now. Barbara Ehrenreich, Deirdre English, Arlie Hochschild, and Barbara Epstein have suggested in various contexts that late twentieth-century capital turned out to be far less invested in the bourgeois family and far harsher than expected.[1] While we can welcome the breakdown of the traditional family, we also need to see the role of capital in breaking it down and ask, as Arlie Hochschild urges us to, if feminism has not in helping its demise aided capital; if while escaping the frying pan of patriarchy we have landed in the fire of market individualism.[2] Hochschild's critique is pointed at bourgeois feminism and its compromises with capital. Without a critique of class or other structural inequalities such as race or nation, bourgeois feminism ends up reproducing exploitive relations, the only difference being that women join men as the beneficiaries. For example, Hochschild and Ehrenreich have shown that the bourgeois woman's dream of "having it all," both a family and a career, is made to come true by the domestic labor of third-world women in an ever-expanding global economy.[3] Certain choices now open to bourgeois women, such as not to marry or have children, can end up being individualistic lifestyle decisions supported by an entire consumer industry.

Fighting for children can provide a vantage point from which we can develop a politics that guides how we live and what we fight for. First, it shifts feminist politics from its grounding in the bourgeois notion of choice—which, after all, assumes a freely choosing subject— to that of need. While the pro-choice stand has fought for and created women's sexual autonomy and is a movement I am committed to and have benefited from, its insistence on choice is individualistic and not structural. It has made it possible for all women to choose to not have children, but the choice to have children—a real choice, that is, that women can give birth knowing that their children will have equal access to the resources of this society—remains unspoken in this discourse. Children need education, health, and housing, intellectual, physical, and emotional nourishment—these are not a choice. To make need the basis of one's politics is to place high social value on those who perform the labor of caregiving, something that has low economic value in capitalism and that patriarchy has undervalued as traditionally done by women.

From a socialist perspective, we need to fight for children because in the idea of childhood we can intuit what a socialist life might be. In capitalism's own youth, when Marx could pay tribute to the revolutionary capabilities of the bourgeoisie, childhood (for all its imprisoning qualities) was a development in that it freed, at least in the imagination, one section of humanity from the market and institutionalized play as children's work. This freedom, socialists hoped, would extend to all as scarcity gave way to abundance, and like children, whose activities are driven by the desire to develop the self, adults would have self-realization as the ultimate goal. For instance, a child who is able to hang from the jungle gym after days of practice goes through the bars over and over again for the sheer pleasure of having extended the range of what her body can do. For Marx, the nonalienated life would, like children's play, be nonspecialized and whole; one would be able to "do one thing today and another tomorrow, to hunt in the morning, fish in the evening, rear cattle in the evening, criticize after dinner, just as I have a mind without ever becoming fisherman, herdsman or critic."[4] Childhood in this imagining was to be extended to all—while capitalism has now extended a market-based childhood responsible for all the cares of adulthood to all, sparing no one from his or her role as worker or consumer.

Childhood also has implicit in it universal humanism that can inform a politics that is collective, a notion under severe attack in the cynical postmodern insistence on difference. In the face of the global inequities, war, and poverty that face children around the world, the postmodern insistence on multiple discourses is a convenient retreat from politics—for instance, Alan Prout and James Alan's claim that "different discursive practices produce different childhoods, each and all of which are 'real' within their own regime of truth."[5] So on what grounds are we to denounce third-world children's labor, when in that culture's regime of truth child labor might be perfectly justified? In its more liberal versions, this discourse produces, Slovej Zizek remarks, Hollywood's logic of plurality, in which all vertical differences that split through society (class or race, for example) are replaced by horizontal ones through which we have to learn to live and accept each other, because they are in actuality complementary.[6] Universality in this view is best achieved through a constant process of translation— a view that is unable to grasp those violent moments when, Zizek reminds us, we realize across the cultural divide that we share the same antagonism.[7] It is a realization we come to when as socialists and feminists we recognize that what is common to our politics is the future of humanity itself.

We have to reclaim childhood to be able to insist on that collective solidarity. Here we can be led by Charlotte Aldebron, a thirteen-year-old opponent of the U.S.—and Britain-led war against Iraq. Speaking at a rally against the war, she asked us to readjust the image we carry in our heads:

> When people think about bombing Iraq, they see a picture in their heads of Saddam Hussein in a military uniform, or maybe soldiers with big black moustaches carrying guns, or the mosaic of George Bush Senior on the lobby floor of the Al-Rashid Hotel with the word "criminal." But guess what? More than half of Iraq's twenty-four million people are children under the age of fifteen. That's twelve million kids. Kids like me. Well, I am almost thirteen, so some are a little older, and some

a lot younger, some boys instead of girls, some with brown hair, not red. But kids who are pretty much like me, just the same. So take a look at me—a good long look. Because I am what you should see in your head when you think about bombing Iraq. I am what you are going to destroy.[8]

In no uncertain terms, Aldebron calls upon us to recognize our humanity by recognizing that children everywhere have the right to a dignified human life.

This book has traced the deconstruction of the notion of childhood in popular U.S. cinema in the last decade of the twentieth century as children are increasingly brought into the market as consumers and as protections previously granted to children by social policy are increasingly withdrawn. Abroad, children lose their lives to war and poverty, as the gulfs between the First and Third Worlds widen. The end of childhood shows the appropriateness of Brecht's understanding that the "peace" provided by capital is only a shade of war:

Their war kills
Whatever their peace
Has left over.[9]

Two centuries of capital have not allowed us to get used to the idea of childhood: that human need, not profit, should guide our decisions; that only collectively can we create a childhood which is truly safe, where children can leave home without fear and come back without anxiety; and that work should for all be like children's play. We must under no circumstances leave out the children. But we should think of them as our collaborators, begin our analysis and action from their vantage point, and not try to push them back into the prison house of the romantic and sentimental notion of children as our Other.

Filmography

Artificial Intelligence. Dir. Steven Spielberg. Dreamworks, Warner, Stanley Kubrick Productions, and Amblin Entertainment, 2001.

Ever After. Dir. Andy Tennant. Perf. Drew Barrymore, Anjelica Huston. Twentieth Century Fox, 1998.

Harry Potter and the Prisoner of Azkaban. Dir. Alfonso Cuarón. Perf. Daniel Radcliffe. Warner Bros., 2004.

Harry Potter and the Sorcerer's Stone. Dir. Chris Columbus. Perf. Daniel Radcliffe. Warner Bros., 2001.

Jack. Dir. Francis Ford Coppola. Perf. Robin Williams. American Zoetrope, Hollywood Pictures, 1996.

Jumanji. Dir. Joe Johnston. Perf. Robin Williams, Bonnie Hunt, Kirsten Dunst. Columbia Pictures, 1995.

A Little Princess. Dir. Alfonso Cuarón. Warner Brothers. 1995.

Little Women. Dir. Gillian Armstrong. Columbia, 1994.

Matilda. Dir. Danny Devito. Perf. Danny Devito, Rhea Perlman, Mara Wilson, Pam Ferris, Embeth Daidtz. Columbia TriStar Films, 1996.

The Matrix. Dir. Andy and Larry Wachowski. Groucho II Film Partnership. Dist. Warner Bros., 1999.

Pocahontas. Dir. Mike Gabriel, Eric Goldberg. Walt Disney Pictures, 1995.

Simple Wish. Dir. Michael Ritchie. Bubble Factory, Universal Pictures, 1997.

Toothless. Dir. Melanie Mayron. Mandenville Films, Walt Disney Television, 1997.

Toy Story. Dir. John Lasseter. Voice Tom Hanks. Walt Disney Pictures, Pixar Animation, 1995.

Toy Story 2. Dir. Ash Brannon and John Lasseter. Walt Disney Pictures, Pixar Animation, 1999.

Notes

INTRODUCTION WITHOUT TRAINING WHEELS

1. Marx, "Capital, Volume I," 376.
2. Corliss, "Hollywood's Kids," 62–65.
3. Zinn, *The Twentieth Century*, 346.
4. Edelstein, "Military Spending Drastically Increases."
5. Zinn, *The Twentieth Century*, 352.
6. Resnick and Wolff, "The Reagan-Bush Strategy," 88–111.
7. For a discussion about the infantilization of the poor under the New Right in the eighties, see Ehrenreich, 183–196.
8. For arguments made in favor of child labor, see Zelizer, *Pricing the Priceless Child*.
9. Kincheloe, "The New Childhood," 174.
10. Zinn, *The Twentieth Century*, 432.
11. See Jameson, *Postmodernism*; Harvey, *The Condition of Postmodernity*.
12. See Kapur, "It's a Small World after All."
13. See Rowbotham, *Hidden from History*; Barrett and McKintosh, *The Anti-social Family*; Hartsock, *Money, Sex, and Power*; Ehrenreich, *Fear of Falling*; Dalla Costa and James, *The Power of Women*; Foreman, *Femininity as Alienation;* Eisenstein, "Developing a Theory."
14. Barrett and McKintosh, *The Anti-social Family*; Coontz, *Social Origins of Private Life*.
15. Hochschild, *The Commercialization of Intimate Life*, 38.
16. See Stacey, "The Family Is Dead."
17. Hochschild, *The Commercialization of Intimate Life*, 185–197. For an advice book that is quite cavalier about using third-world women's labor, see Sherman, *A Housekeeper Is Cheaper*.
18. Marx, "Capital, Volume I," 373.
19. Benjamin, "One-Way Street," 69.
20. Marx, "Capital, Volume I," 415
21. Jameson, "Totality as Conspiracy," 9–10.

22. Benjamin, "A Berlin Chronicle," 28.
23. Harvey, *The Condition of Postmodernity*, 61.

CHAPTER 1 CRADLE TO GRAVE

1. See Adorno and Horkheimer, "The Culture Industry"; Winn, *The Plug-in Drug*; Postman, *The Disappearance of Childhood*; Kline, *Out of The Garden*.
2. Seiter, *Sold Separately*; also see Seiter, *Television and New Media Audiences*. Buckingham, *Moving Images*; also see Buckingham, *Small Screen*.
3. Schneider, *Children's Television*, 2.
4. Guber and Berry, *Marketing to and through Kids*, 3; David Vogel, president of Walt Disney Pictures, the family division of the studio, quoted in Bernard Weinraub, "Fun for the Whole Family: Movies for Children, and Their Parents, Are Far from 'Pollyanna,'" *New York Times*, July 22, 1997, Living Arts section.
5. See Wullschlager, *Inventing Wonderland*; Carpenter, *Secret Gardens*.
6. Keith, "The Marketing Revolution," 47.
7. Larson, *The Naked Consumer*, 23.
8. Ibid., 26.
9. Marx, *Economic and Philosophical Manuscripts*, 94.
10. Larson, *The Naked Consumer*, 5.
11. Schneider, *Children's Television*, 9.
12. Hirschman and Holbrook, *Postmodern Consumer Research*, 18.
13. Larson, *The Naked Consumer*, 175.
14. Del Vecchio, *Creating Ever-Cool*, 24.
15. Leonhardt and Kerwin, "Hey Kid."
16. McNeal, *Kids as Customers*, 93.
17. See Jenkins, "The Sensuous Child; Ehrenreich, *Fear of Falling*.
18. Schneider, *Children's Television*, 22.
19. Schickel, *The Disney Version*, 18.
20. Baudrillard, "For a Critique," 31.
21. Leonhardt and Kerwin, "Hey Kid," 48.
22. Schneider, *Children's Television*, 29.
23. See Cross, *Kids' Stuff*.
24. Schneider quotes Minow in *Children's Television*, 169.
25. "FCC Won't Force Children's Programs," *Boston Globe*, February 12, 1983.
26. Giddens, *The Consequences of Modernity*, 49.
27. Winn, *The Plug-in Drug*, 209; Kline, *Out of the Garden*, 3.
28. Winn, *The Plug-in Drug*, 201.
29. Ibid., 204.
30. Dahl, *Charlie and the Chocolate Factory*, 141.
31. Cross, *Kids' Stuff*, 231
32. Benjamin, "A Berlin Chronicle," 40.
33. Harvey, *The Condition of Postmodernity*, 61.

CHAPTER 2 LOST KINGDOMS

1. Carroll, *Through the Looking Glass*, 158.
2. Carroll, *Alice's Adventures in Wonderland*, xii.
3. For an excellent biography of the complex life of Burnett, see Gretchen Holbrook Gerzina, *Frances Hodgson Burnett: The Unexpected Life of the Author of the Secret Garden* (New Brunswick, N.J., and London: Rutgers University Press. 2004).
4. There is a significant body of literature that analyzes the works of these

classical nineteenth- and early twentieth-century children's writers that includes Carpenter, *Secret Gardens*; Rose, *The Case of Peter Pan*; and Wullschlager, *Inventing Wonderland*.

5. Carpenter, *Secret Gardens*, 8–9.
6. Carroll, quoted in Wullschlager, *Inventing Wonderland*, 21.
7. Burnett. *The Little Princess*, 213–214. Succeeding references to page numbers in this book appear in parentheses in the text.
8. Carroll, *Alice in Wonderland*, 12.
9. See Metz, *The Imaginary Signifier*.
10. Green is quoted in Parkinson, *The Graham Greene Film Reader*, 234; also see 449–452.
11. Chaplin, *Photoplay*, December 1923, quoted in Howe, "What's Going to Happen," 60.
12. Moore, *Twinkle, Twinkle, Little Star*, 83.
13. See Moore, *Twinkle, Twinkle, Little Star*; Cary, *Hollywood's Children;* Strait, *Hollywood's Children*.
14. Moore, *Twinkle, Twinkle, Little Star*, 126–128. Cary, *Hollywood's Children*, 114–115.
15. On Shirley Temple, see Gross, *Kids' Stuff*, 117; on Baby Peggy and Jane Withers, see Moore, *Twinkle, Twinkle, Little Star*, 200, 206.
16. Moore, *Twinkle, Twinkle, Little Star*, ix.
17. The Laxman Rekha set up the boundaries that Sita was not supposed to cross without Rama or Laxman. In the Ramayana, Sita crosses that circle to give alms to a beggar, actually Ravana in disguise, who kidnaps her.
18. Lesage, "Women's Fragmented Consciousness," 329.
19. Buck-Morss, *The Dialectics of Seeing*, 117.
20. Williams, *Lost Icons*, 11–12.

CHAPTER 3 OF COWBOYS AND INDIANS

The chapter epigraph is quoted in Jeffrey Mehlman, *Walter Benjamin for Children: An Essay on His Radio Years* (Chicago: University of Chicago Press, 1993), 5.

1. See Jameson, *Postmodernism*; Habermas, "Modernity, an Incomplete Project."
2. Eagleton, *The Illusions of Postmodernism*, 51.
3. Benjamin, "Theses on the Philosophy of History," 254.
4. Ibid., 255.
5. Robert Eaglestaff, interview by Michael Kilian, "Pocahontas' Tale," *Chicago Tribune*, July 2, 1995.
6. Zinn, *A People's History*, 13.
7. Sobchack, "Introduction," 6.
8. Carol Johnston, "A Luscious Babe, but Politically Correct," review of *Pocahontas*, *Wall Street Journal*, July 12, 1995.
9. "Coming to Classrooms: The Real Pocahontas Story," *New York Times*, July 12, 1995.
10. See Eisenstein, "Developing a Theory."
11. Young, *The Mother of Us All*, 395, quotes from John Smith, *True Relation of 1608*, in *Narratives of Early Virginia, 1606–1625*, ed. Gardiner Tyler (New York: Charles Scribner's Sons, 1907), 27–71.
12. Benjamin, "The Storyteller," 102.
13. Barthes, *Mythologies*, 54–55.
14. Benjamin, "One-Way Street," 69.

CHAPTER 4 OBSOLESCENCE AND OTHER PLAYROOM
ANXIETIES

1. Marx, "Capital, Volume 1," 319.
2. Marx, "Alienation and Social Classes," 134.
3. Williams, *The Velveteen Rabbit*, 4. Succeeding references to page numbers in this book appear in parentheses in the text.
4. Marx, "Capital, Volume 3," 441.
5. Phillips, *The Beast in the Nursery*, xix.
6. Freud, *The Sexual Enlightenment of Children*, 22.
7. Phillips, *The Beast in the Nursery*, xx..
8. Adorno and Horkheimer, "The Culture Industry," 29.
9. Bodnar, "Awesome Bucks for Kids' Junk," 47.
10. Fox and Fox, *Beanie Baby Handbook*, 23.
11. Jodi Wilgoren, "The Children's Defense Fund: After Welfare, Working Poor Still Struggle, Report Finds," *New York Times,* April 25, 2002.

CHAPTER 5 THE CHILDREN WHO NEED NO PARENTS

1. Baudrillard, *Symbolic Exchange and Death*, 18.
2. Clarke, *Childhood's End*, 189.
3. Holt, *Escape from Childhood*, 172.
4. Presser is quoted in Carol Kleiman, "Odd Hours: Moving to an Around-the-Clock Economy," *Chicago Tribune*, January 28, 1996.
5. See Davis-Floyd and Dumit, *Cyborg Babies*.
6. Kinder, *Playing with Power in Movies,* 115
7. Marx, "Capital, Volume 1," 376.
8. Marx, "Economic and Philosophic Manuscripts," 91.

CHAPTER 6 THE BURDENS OF TIME IN THE BOURGEOIS
PLAYROOM

1. For Marx, boredom was the impetus that would move the Hegelian thinker from following the abstract history of the absolute idea, as if ideas had a life of their own, to beginning to intuit, that is, beginning to contemplate through an awareness of the senses the material foundations of ideas. It is then no stretch to suggest that Marx would have seen boredom also as the impetus that could move the alienated consumer to unlock the illusory nature of the fabricated attractions of consumer culture.
2. Spacks, *Boredom*, 13.
3. See Seo, "The Shock of Boredom." I benefited enormously from Seo's insights, and this chapter is basically a spin-off of his work.
4. Kracauer, "Boredom," 334.
5. Baudelaire is quoted in Lafourgue, *The Defeat of Baudelaire*, 43.
6. Phillips, *On Kissing*, 69.
7. Hitchcock, *Haunted Houseful*, iii.
8. Benjamin, "The Storyteller," 91.
9. In Northbrook, a primarily white upper-class Chicago suburb, several high school seniors, including girls, beat juniors and showered them with mud and feces, injuring five girls seriously enough to send them to the hospital, all the time videotaping the incident (*Southern Illinoisan*, May 13, 2003, 1).

10. Friedberg, *Window Shopping*, 142, 143.
11. See Wilson, *The Sphinx in the City*; Peiss, "Commercial Pleasure"; Busch, *For Fun and Profit*.
12. Goulart, *The Assault on Childhood*, 3.
13. Grossberg, *We Gotta Get Out*, 183.
14. Meyerowitz, *No Sense of Place*, 227.
15. Ivy, "'Have You Seen Me?'" 95.
16. Hochschild, *The Commercialization of Intimate Life*, 13–29.
17. See Kern, *The Culture of Time and Space*, 94.
18. Jameson, *Postmodernism*, 285.
19. Baudrillard, "The Virtual Illusion," 97.
20. Marx, "Economic and Philosophic Manuscripts," 91.

CHAPTER 7 FREE MARKET, BRANDED IMAGINATION

1. I wish to thank my daughter, Suhaila, and her fifth-grade class for an in-depth discussion of Harry Potter, and I dedicate this chapter to their teacher, Michelle Kornreich, who empowered them, teaching them to think critically and imagine differently.
2. Todd McCarthy, "Wizard of Awes Will Conjure Gigantic B.B," *Variety*, November 12–18, 2001, 27.
3. Wasser, *Veni, Vidi, Video*, 168.
4. Dan Ackman, "Harry Potter Is a Fraud," *www.forbes.com/2001/11/19/1119topnews.html*.
5. Wasser, *Veni, Vidi, Video*, 167.
6. Ackman, "Harry Potter Is a Fraud."
7. Ibid.
8. "Harry Potter and the Wacky Web," ZDNET News, July 6, 2000. *http://zdnet.com.com/2100-11_2-522027.html*.
9. A Google search for "HarryPotter" turns up adult fan sites that interpret Harry Potter as a gay icon.
10. Rowling, *Harry Potter and the Sorcerer's Stone*, 1. Succeeding references to page numbers in this book appear in parentheses in the text.
11. See *web.ukonline.co.uk/bringers/temp/c–potter.html#news*.
12. See the excellent article by Albom, "Young Fans' Web Sites," which quotes the Warner Bros. letter.
13. See *www.dprophet.com/dada/manifesto.html*.

CONCLUSION ALL THAT IS SOLID MELTS INTO AIR

1. See the introduction for a detailed discussion of the harshness of late twentieth-century capitalism.
2. Hochschild, *The Commercialization of Intimate Life*, 145.
3. Ehrenreich and Hochschild, *Global Women*.
4. Marx, "The German Ideology," 160
5. Prout and Alan, "A New Paradigm," 7.
6. Zizek, *Welcome to the Desert*, 64–65.
7. Ibid., 66.
8. Charlotte Aldebron, "What about Iraqi Children?" *WireTap*, March 3, 2003, *www.wiretapmag.org/story.htm?StoryID=15291*.
9. Brecht, "Those at the Top Say," 288.

Bibliography

Adorno, Theodore, and Max Horkheimer. "The Culture Industry: Enlighten-
ment as Mass Deception." In *Cultural Studies Reader*, ed. Simon During.
(Extracted from *Dialectic of Enlightenment*, trans. John Cumming.) London:
Routledge, 1993, 29–43.

Albom, Mitch. "Young Fans' Web Sites Become a Big Harry Deal." *Jewish World
Review*, March 5, 2001/10 Adar, 5761. Available on *www.jewishworldreview.
com/0301/albom030501.asp*

Allen, Robert. "Home Alone Together: Hollywood and the 'Family Film.'" In
Identifying Hollywood's Audiences: Cultural Identity and the Movies, ed.
Melvyn Stokes and Richard Maltby. London: BFI Publishing, 1999, 109–
134.

Aries, Phillipe. *Centuries of Childhood: A Social History of Family Life*. Translated by Robert Baldick. New York: Knopf, 1962.

Banks, Lynne Reid. *The Indian in the Cupboard*. New York: Avon Books, 1980.

Barrett, Michelle, and Mary McIntosh. *The Anti-social Family*. 2d ed. London:
Verso, 1991.

Barthes, Roland. *Mythologies*. Paris: Editions du Seuil, 1957. Reprint, New York:
Hill and Wang, 1972.

Baudrillard, Jean. "For a Critique of the Political Economy of the Sign." In *Jean
Baudrillard: Selected Writings*, ed. Mark Poster. Cambridge: Stanford University Press, 1988, 31

———. *For a Critique of the Political Economy of the Sign*. Translated by Charles
Levin. St. Louis: Telos, 1981.

———. *Symbolic Exchange and Death*. Translated by Iain Hamilton Grant. Thousand Oaks, Calif.: Sage, 1998, 18.

———. "The Virtual Illusion: Or the Automatic Writing of the World." *Theory,
Culture, and Society* 12, 4 (1995): 97–107.

Benjamin, Walter. "A Berlin Chronicle." In *Reflections: Essays, Aphorisms,
Autobiographical Writings*, ed. Peter Demetz, trans. Edmund Jephcott. New
York: Schocken Books, 1978, 3–60.

———. "Berliner Spielzeugwanderung II in Aufklarung fur Kinder." Quoted in Jeffrey Mehlman, *Walter Benjamin for Children: An Essay on His Radio Years.* Chicago: University of Chicago Press, 1993.

———. Conversations with Brecht. In *Reflections: Essays, Aphorisms, Autobiographical Writings*, ed. Peter Demetz, trans. Edmund Jephcott. New York: Schocken Books, 1978, 203–219.

———. "One-Way Street." In *Reflections: Essays, Aphorisms, Autobiographical Writings*, ed. Peter Demetz, trans. Edmund Jephcott. New York: Schocken Books, 1978, 61–96.

———. "The Storyteller." In *Illuminations: Walter Benjamin, Essays and Reflections*, ed. Hannah Arendt, trans. Harry Zohn. New York: Schocken Books, 1968, 83–110.

———. "Theses on the Philosophy of History." In *Illuminations: Walter Benjamin, Essays and Reflections*, ed. Hanna Arendt. New York: Schocken Books, 1968.

Bettelheim, Bruno. *The Uses of Enchantment: The Meaning and Importance of Fairy Tales.* New York: Vintage Books, 1977.

Bodnar, Janet. "Awesome Bucks for Kids' Junk: Collect for Love, and the Money May Follow." *Kiplinger's Personal Finance Magazine* 47, 4 (April 1993): 79.

Brecht, Bertolt. "Those at the Top Say: Peace and War." In *Bertolt Brecht Poems: 1913–1956*, ed. Jon Willet and Ralph Manheim. London: Methuen, 1976, 288.

Buckingham, David. *Moving Images: Understanding Children's Emotional Responses to Television.* London: Manchester University Press, 1996.

———. *Small Screens: Television for Children.* Leicester, Eng.: Leicester University Press, 2002.

Buck-Morss, Susan. *The Dialectics of Seeing: Walter Benjamin and the Arcades Project.* Cambridge: MIT Press, 1995.

Burnett, Frances Hodgson. *Little Lord Fauntleroy.* Illustrations from drawings by Reginald B. Birch. New York: Scribner, 1886.

———. *The Little Princess.* New York: Platt and Munk, 1905. Reprint, London: Puffin Books, 1961.

———. *The Secret Garden.* New York: Grosset and Dunlap, 1911. Reprint, London: Puffin Books, 1994.

Cagle, Jess. "The First Look at Harry." *Time*, November 5, 2001. *www.time.com/time/2001/harrypotter/story.html.*

Carpenter, Humphrey. *Secret Gardens: A Study of the Golden Age of Children's Literature.* Boston: Houghton Mifflin, 1985.

Carroll, Lewis. *Alice's Adventures in Wonderland.* 1865. New York: Holt, Rinehart and Winston, 1923.

Cary, Diane Serra. *Hollywood's Children: An Inside Account of the Child Star Era.* Boston: Houghton Mifflin, 1978.

Clarke, Arthur C. *Childhood's End.* New York: Ballantine Books, 1953.

Collodi, Carlo. *The Adventures of Pinocchio.* Translated by M. A. Murray. London: Fischer Unwin, 1892. Reprint, New York: Grosset and Dunlap, 1965.

Comaroff, Jean, and John Comaroff. "Africa Observed: Discourses of the Imperial Imagination." In *Of Revelation and Revolution: Christianity, Colonialism, and Consciousness in South Africa*, ed. Comaroff and Comaroff. Vol. 1. Chicago: University of Chicago Press, 1991, 86–126.

Coontz, Stephanie. *The Social Origins of Private Life: A History of American Families, 1600–1900.* London and New York: Verso, 1988.

———. *The Way We Never Were: American Families and the Nostalgia Trap.* New York: Basic Books, 1992.

Corliss, Richard. "Hollywood's Kids." *Time*, June 28, 1993, 62–65.

Cross, Gary. *Kids' Stuff: Toys and the Changing World of American Childhood.* Cambridge: Harvard University Press, 1997.

Cunningham, Hugh. *Children and Childhood in Western Society since 1500.* London and New York: Longman, 1995.

Dahl, Roald. *Charlie and the Chocolate Factory.* New York: Knopf, 1964.

Dalla Costa, M., and Selma James. *The Power of Women and the Subversion of the Community.* Bristol, Eng.: Falling Wall Press, 1975.

Davis-Floyd, Robbie, and Joseph Dumit, eds. *Cyborg Babies: From Techno-Sex to Techno Tots.* New York: Routledge, 1998.

Del Vecchio, Gene. *Creating Ever-Cool: A Marketer's Guide to a Kid's Heart.* Gretna, La.: Pelican Publishing, 1997

DeMause, Lloyd. *The History of Childhood.* New York: Psychohistory Press, 1974.

D'Entremont, John. "Pocahontas: Motion Picture Review." *Journal of American History* 82 (December 1995): 1302–1305.

Dyer, Richard. "Heavenly Bodies: Film Stars and Society." *Film and Theory: An Anthology*, ed. Robert Stam and Toby Miller. Cambridge, Mass.: Blackwell, 2000, 603–617.

Eagleton, Terry. *The Illusions of Postmodernism.* London: Blackwell, 1996.

Eckert, Charles. "Shirley Temple and the House of Rockefeller." In *American Media and Mass Culture: Left Perspectives*, ed. Donald Lazare. Berkeley: University of California Press, 1987, 164–177.

Edelstein, Jodi. "Military Spending Drastically Increases in FY 2003." *Vanderbilt Orbis*, November 20, 2002. *http://www.vaderbiltorbis.com*

Ehrenreich, Barbara. *Fear of Falling: The Inner Life of the Middle Class.* New York: Harper Perennial, 1989.

———. "Life without Father: Reconsidering Socialist-Feminist Theory." In *Women, Class, and the Feminist Imagination: A Socialist-Feminist Reader*, ed. Karen V. Hansen and Ilene J. Philipson. Philadelphia: Temple University Press, 1990, 268–276.

Ehrenreich, Barbara, and Arlie Russell Hochschild, eds. *Global Women: Nannies, Maids, and Sex Workers in the New Economy.* New York: Metropolitan Books, 2002.

Eisenstein, Zillah. "Developing a Theory of Capitalist Patriarchy and Socialist Feminism." In *Capitalist Patriarchy and the Case for Socialist Feminism*, ed. Eisenstein. New York: Monthly Review Press, 1979, 5–40.

Enis, Ben M., and Keith Cox, eds. *Marketing Classics: A Selection of Influential Articles.* 4th ed. Toronto: Allyn and Bacon, 1981.

Ewen, Stuart, and Elizabeth Ewen. *Channels of Desire: Mass Images and the Shaping of American Consciousness.* New York: McGraw Hill, 1982.

Fabian, Johannes. *Time and the Other: How Anthropology Makes its Object.* New York: Columbia University Press, 1983.

Fagan, Jeffrey, and Valerie West. "The Decline of the Juvenile Death Penalty: Scientific Evidence of Evolving Norms." *Journal of Criminal Law and Criminology* (forthcoming).

Foreman, Anne. *Femininity as Alienation: Women in Marxism and Psychoanalysis.* London: Pluto, 1977.

Fox, Les, and Sue Fox. *The Beanie Baby Handbook.* Midland Park, N.J.: West Highland Publishing, 1997.

Fox, Roy F. *Harvesting Minds.* Westport, Conn., and London: Praeger, 1996.

Fraad, Harriet, Stephen Resnick, and Richard Wolff. *Bringing It All Back Home:*

Class, Gender, and Power in the Modern Household. London: Pluto Press, 1994.

Freud, Sigmund. *The Sexual Enlightenment of Children*. New York: Collier Books, 1963.

Friedberg, Anne. *Window Shopping: Cinema and the Postmodern*. Berkeley: University of California Press, 1993.

Giddens, Anthony. *The Consequences of Modernity*. Stanford, Calif.: Stanford University Press, 1990.

———. *The Transformation of Intimacy*. Stanford, Calif.: Stanford University Press, 1992.

Goulart, Ron. *The Assault on Childhood*. Los Angeles: Sherbourne, 1969.

Green, Rayna. "The Pocahontas Perplex: The Image of Indian Women in American Culture." *Massachusetts Review* (Autumn 1975): 698–714.

Grossberg, Lawrence. *We Gotta Get Out of This Place: Popular Conservatism and Postmodern Culture*. New York and London: Routledge, 1992.

Guber, Selina S., and Jon Berry. *Marketing to and through Kids*. New York: McGraw Hill, 1993.

Gunning, Tom. "The World as Object Lesson: Cinema Audiences, Visual Culture, and the St. Louis Fair, 1904." *Film History* 6 (1994): 422–444.

Habermas, Jurgen. "Modernity, an Incomplete Project." In *The Anti-Aesthetic*, ed. Hal Foster. New York: New Press, 1983, 3–15.

Hansen, Miriam. "Of Mice and Ducks: Benjamin and Adorno on Disney." *South Atlantic Quarterly* 92, 1 (Winter 1993): 27–61.

Hartsock, Nancy. *Money, Sex, and Power: Towards a Feminist Historical Materialism*. New York: Longman, 1983.

Harvey, David. *The Condition of Postmodernity: An Inquiry into the Origins of Cultural Change*. Cambridge, Mass.: Blackwell, 1990.

Hawking, Stephen. *A Brief History of Time*. New York: Bantam Books, 1988.

Higonnet, Anne. *Pictures of Innocence: The History and Crisis of Ideal Childhood*. London: Thames and Hudson, 1998.

Hirschman, Elizabeth, and Morris Holbrook. *Postmodern Consumer Research: The Study of Consumption as Text*. London: Sage, 1992, 18.

Hitchcock, Alfred. *Haunted Houseful*. New York: Barnes and Noble, 1961.

Hochschild, Arlie. *The Commercialization of Intimate Life: Notes from Home and Work*. Berkeley: University of California Press, 2003.

Holt, John. *Escape From Childhood*. New York: E. P. Dutton, 1974.

Howe, Herbert. "What's Going to Happen to Jackie Coogan." *Photoplay*, December 1923. Quoted in Cary, *Hollywood's Children*.

Ivy, Marlyn. "'Have You Seen Me?' Recovering the Inner Child in Late Twentieth-Century America." In *Children and the Politics of Culture*, ed. Sharon Stephens. Princeton, N.J.: Princeton University Press, 1995, 79–103.

Jameson, Fredric. *The Political Unconscious: Narrative as a Socially Symbolic Act*. Ithaca, N.Y.: Cornell University Press, 1981.

———. *Postmodernism, or the Cultural Logic of Late Capitalism*. Durham, N.C.: Duke University Press, 1991.

———. "Totality as Conspiracy." *The Geopolitical Aesthetic: Cinema and Space in the World System*. Bloomington and Indianapolis: Indiana University Press, 1995, 9–10.

Jenkins, Henry. "The Sensuous Child: Benjamin Spock and the Sexual Revolution." In *The Children's Culture Reader*, ed. Jenkins. New York: New York University Press, 1998, 209–230.

Kapur, Jyotsna. "Children out of Control: The Debate on Children and Television in Late Twentieth Century America." In *Kids Media Culture*, ed. Marsha Kinder. Durham, N.C., and London: Duke University Press, 1999, 122–138.

———. "It's a Small World after All: Globalization and the Transformation of Childhood in India." *Visual Anthropology* 11 (1998; special issue on Indian film and television): 387–397.

Keith, Robert. "The Marketing Revolution." In *Marketing Classics: A Selection of Influential Articles*, ed. Ben M. Enis and Keith Cox. 4th ed. Toronto: Allyn and Bacon, 1981, 44–49.

Kern, Stephen. *The Culture of Time and Space: 1880–1918*. Cambridge: Harvard University Press, 1983, 94.

Kincaid, James R. "Producing Erotic Children." In *The Children's Culture Reader*, ed. Henry Jenkins. New York: New York University Press, 1998, 241–253.

Kincheloe, Joe L. "The New Childhood: Home Alone as a Way of Life." In *The Children's Culture Reader*, ed. Henry Jenkins. New York: New York University Press, 1998, 159–177.

Kinder, Marsha. *Playing with Power in Movies, Television, and Video Games: From Muppet Babies to Teenage Mutant Ninja Turtles*. Berkeley: University of California Press, 1991.

Klein, Naomi. *No Logo*. Toronto: Vintage, 2000.

Kline, Steven. *Out of the Garden: Toys, TV, and Children's Culture in the Age of Marketing*. London: Verso, 1993.

Kracauer, Seigfried. "Boredom." In *The Mass Ornament*, ed and trans. Thomas Y. Levin. Cambridge and London: Harvard University Press, 1995, 331–334.

Kraus, Robert. *Another Mouse to Feed*. New York: Simon and Schuster, 1980.

Kuhn, Reinhard. *The Demon of Noontide: Ennui in Western Literature*. New York: Columbia University Press, 1984.

Lafourgue, Ren. *The Defeat of Baudelaire: A Psycho-analytical Study of the Neurosis of Charles Baudelaire*. Translated by Herbert Agar. London: Leonard and Virginia Woolf, 1932.

Larson, Erik. *The Naked Consumer: How Our Private Lives Became Public Commodities*. New York: Penguin Books, 1992.

Latham, Rob. *Consuming Youth: Vampires, Cyborgs, and the Culture of Consumption*. Chicago: University of Chicago Press, 2002.

Leonhardt, David, and Kathleen Kerwin. "Hey Kid, Buy This!" *Business Week*, June 30, 1997, 61–67.

Lesage, Julia. "Women's Fragmented Consciousness in Feminist Experimental Autobiographical Video." In *Feminism and Documentary*, ed. Diane Waldman and Janet Walker. Minneapolis and London: University of Minnesota Press, 1999, 309–338.

Marx, Karl. "Alienation and Social Classes (from 'The Holy Family')." Translated by Robert Tucker. In *The Marx-Engels Reader*, ed. Robert Tucker. 2d ed. New York: W. W. Norton, 1978, 133–135.

———. "Capital, Volume 1." Edited by Friedrich Engles, translated by Samuel Moore and Edward Aveling. In *The Marx-Engels Reader*, ed. Robert Tucker. 2d ed. New York: W. W. Norton, 1978, 294–438.

———. "Capital, Volume 3." Translated by Samuel Moore and Edward Aveling. In *The Marx-Engels Reader*, ed. Robert Tucker. 2d ed. New York: W. W. Norton, 1978, 439–442.

———. "Economic and Philosophic Manuscripts." Translated by Martin Milligan. In *The Marx Engels Reader*, ed. Robert Tucker. 2d ed. New York: W. W. Norton, 1978, 66–125.

———. "The German Ideology." Translated by Martin Milligan. In *The Marx-Engels Reader*, ed. Robert Tucker. 2d ed. New York: W. W. Norton, 1978, 146–202.

May, Elaine Tyler. *Homeward Bound: American Families in the Cold War Era.* New York: Basic Books, 1988.

McNeal, James. *Kids as Customers: A Handbook of Marketing to Children.* New York: Lexington Press, 1992.

Meehan, Eileen. "Commodity Audience, Actual Audience: The Blindspot Debate." In *Illuminating the Blindspots: Essays Honoring Dallas W. Smythe,* ed. Janet Wasko, Vincent Mosco, and Manjunath Pendakur. Norwood, N.J.: Ablex, 1993, 378–400.

Metz, Christian. *The Imaginary Signifier: Psychoanalysis and the Cinema.* Translated by Celia Britton, Annwyl Williams, Ben Brewster, and Alfred Guzzitti. Bloomington: Indiana University Press, 1982.

Meyerowitz, Joshua. *No Sense of Place: The Impact of the Electronic Media on Social Behavior.* New York: Oxford University Press, 1985.

Moore, Dick. *Twinkle, Twinkle, Little Star but Don't Have Sex and Don't Take the Car.* New York: Harper and Row, 1984.

Mulvey, Laura. "Visual Pleasure and Narrative Cinema." In *Film Theory and Criticism: Introductory Readings*, ed. Leo Braudy and Marshall Cohen. 5th ed. New York: Oxford University Press, 1999, 833–844.

National Labor Committee. *Toys of Misery: A Report on the Toy Industry in China.* Preface by Charles Kernaghan. December 2001. *www.nlcnet.org.*

Parkinson, David, ed. *The Graham Greene Film Reader: Reviews, Essays, Interviews, and Film Stories.* New York: Applause Theater Book Publishers, 1995.

Paul, William. *Laughing Screaming: Modern Hollywood Horror and Comedy.* New York: Columbia University Press, 1997.

Pearson, Ruth, and Diane Elson. *Women's Employment and Multinationals in Europe.* Basingstoke, Eng.: Macmillan, 1989.

Peiss, Kathy. "Commercial Pleasure and the 'Women's Question.'" In *For Fun and Profit: The Transformation of Leisure into Consumption*, ed. Richard Busch. Philadelphia: Temple University Press, 1986.

Philipson, Ilene J. "Heterosexual Antagonisms and the Politics of Mothering." In *Women, Class, and the Feminist Imagination*, ed. Karen V. Hansen and Ilene J. Philipson. Philadelphia: Temple University Press, 1990.

Phillips, Adam. *The Beast in the Nursery: On Curiosity and Other Appetites.* New York: Vintage Books, 1998.

———. *On Kissing, Tickling, and Being Bored: Psychoanalytic Essays on the Unexamined Life.* Cambridge: Harvard University Press, 1994.

Phizacklea, Annie, and Carol Wolkowitz. *Homeworking Women.* London: Sage Publications, 1995.

Plumb, J. H. *The Birth of a Consumer Society: The Commercialization of Eighteenth-Century England.* Bloomington: Indiana University Press, 1982.

Poster, Mark. *Critical Theory of the Family.* New York: Seabury, 1978.

Postman, Neil. *The Disappearance of Childhood.* New York: Vintage Books, 1982.

Press, Eyal. "Barbie's Betrayal: The Toy Industry's Broken Workers." *The Nation*, December 30, 1996, 12.

Prout, Alan, and James Alan. "A New Paradigm for the Sociology of Childhood? Provenance, Promise, and Problems." In *Constructing and Reconstructing Childhood*, ed. Prout and Alan. London: Falmer Press, 1990, 7–35.

Rand, Erica. *Barbie's Queer Accessories.* Durham, N.C., and London: Duke University Press, 1995.

Resnick, Stephen, and Richard Wolff. "The Reagan-Bush Strategy: Shifting Crisis from Enterprises to Households." In *Bringing It All Back Home: Class, Gender, and Power in the Modern Household,* ed. Harriet Fraad, Resnick, and Wolff. London: Pluto Press, 1994, 88–111.

Rist, Ray. *The Urban School: A Factory for Failure. A Study of Education in American Society.* Cambridge: MIT Press, 1973.

Robertson, Karen. "Pocahontas at the Masque." *Signs: Journal of Women in Culture and Society* 21, 31 (Spring 1996): 551–583.

Rose, Jacqueline. *The Case of Peter Pan, or the Impossibility of Children's Fiction.* London: Macmillan, 1984.

Rousseau, Jean-Jacques. *Emile, or On Education.* Translated and with an introduction by Alan Bloom. New York: Basic Books, 1979.

Rowbotham, Sheila. *Hidden from History: Rediscovering Women in History from the Seventeenth Century to the Present.* New York: Pantheon Books, 1975.

Rowling, J. K. *Harry Potter and the Sorcerer's Stone.* New York: Scholastic Press, 1997.

Said, Edward. *Orientalism.* New York: Pantheon Books, 1978.

Schickel, Richard. *The Disney Version: The Life, Times, Art, and Commerce of Walt Disney.* New York: Simon and Schuster, 1968.

Schneider, Cy. *Children's Television: The Art, the Business, and How It Works.* Chicago: NTC Books, 1987.

Seiter, Ellen. *Sold Separately: Children and Parents in Consumer Culture.* New Brunswick, N.J.: Rutgers University Press, 1991.

———. *Television and New Media Audiences.* New York: Oxford University Press, 1999.

Seo, Hyunsuk. "The Shock of Boredom: The Aesthetics of Absence, Futility, and Bliss in Moving Images." Ph.D. diss., Northwestern University, 2002.

Sherman, Kathy Fitzgerald. *A Housekeeper Is Cheaper than a Divorce: Why You Can Afford to Hire Help and How to Get It.* Mountain View, Calif.: Life Tools Press, 2000.

Smythe, Dallas. "Communications: Blindspot of Western Marxism." *Canadian Journal of Political and Social Theory* 2, 3 (1997): 1–27.

Sobchack, Vivian. "Introduction: History Happens." In *The Persistence of History: Cinema, Television, and the Modern Event,* ed. Sobchack. New York: Routledge, 1996.

Spacks, Patricia Meyer. *Boredom: The Literary History of a State of Mind.* Chicago and London: University of Chicago Press, 1995.

Spigel, Lynn. *Make Room for TV: Television and the Family Ideal in Postwar America.* Chicago: University of Chicago Press, 1992.

Stacey, Judith. "The Family Is Dead, Long Live Our Families." In *The Socialist Feminist Project: A Contemporary Reader in Theory and Politics,* ed. Nancy Holstrom. New York: Monthly Review Press, 2002, 90–101.

Staiger, Janet. "The Package-Unit System: Unit Management after 1955." In *The Classical Hollywood Cinema: Film Style and Mode of Production to 1960,* ed. David Bordwell, Staiger, and Kirsten Thompson. New York: Columbia University Press, 1985.

Strait, Raymond. *Hollywood's Children.* New York: St. Martin's Press, 1982.

Sutton-Smith, Brian. *Toys as Culture.* New York: Gardner Press, 1986.

Van Allsburg, Chris. *Jumanji.* New York: Houghton Mifflin, 1981.

Wasko, Janet. The Magical-Market of Disney. *Monthly Review* 52, 11 (2003): 56–71.

Wasser, Fredrick. *Veni, Vidi, Video*. Austin: University of Texas Press, 1998.

Williams, Margery. *The Velveteen Rabbit, or How Toys Become Real*. New York: George H. Doran, 1922. New York: Holt, 1983.

Williams, Rowan. *Lost Icons: Reflections on Cultural Bereavement*. London: Morehouse, 2000.

Willis, Susan. *A Primer for Daily Living*. London: Routledge, 1991.

Wilson, Elizabeth. *The Sphinx in the City: Urban Life, the Control of Disorder, and Women*. Berkeley and Los Angeles: University of California Press, 1991.

Winn, Marie. *The Plug-in Drug*. New York: Viking, 1977.

Wullschlager, Jackie. *Inventing Wonderland: The Lives and Fantasies of Lewis Carroll, Edward Lear, J. M. Barrie, Kenneth Grahame, and A. A. Milne*. New York: Free Press, 1995.

Wyatt, Justin. *High Concept: Movies and Marketing in Hollywood*. Austin: University of Texas Press, 1994.

Young, Philip. "The Mother of Us All: Pocahontas Reconsidered." *Kenyon Review* 24, 3 (Summer 1962): 391–441.

Zelizer, Viviana A. *Pricing the Priceless Child: The Changing Social Value of Children*. New York: Basic Books, 1985.

Zinn, Howard. *A People's History of the United States, 1492–Present*. New York: Harper Perennial, 1995.

———. *The Twentieth Century: A People's History*. Revised and Updated. New York: Harper Perennial, 1998.

Zipes, Jack. *Breaking the Magic Spell: Radical Theories of Folk and Fairy Tales*. Austin: University of Texas Press, 1979.

Zizek, Slovej. *Welcome to the Desert of the Real*. London: Verso, 2002.

Index

About the Author

JYOTSNA KAPUR teaches in the department of cinema and photography at Southern Illinois University. She was born in India and has studied in India and the United States. Her research and teaching interests center on the integration of media culture and industry with global capital and on the ways that integration translates into how we experience life. She lives in Carbondale, Illinois, with her two children.